Size, Growth, Profits and Executive Compensation in the Large Corporation

Also by David J. Smyth
THE DEMAND FOR FARM MACHINERY
  (*with H. G. Scott*)
FORECASTING THE UNITED KINGDOM ECONOMY
  (*with J. C. K. Ash*)

Size, Growth, Profits and Executive Compensation in the Large Corporation:

A Study of the 500 Largest United Kingdom and United States Industrial Corporations

David J. Smyth, William J. Boyes and
Dennis E. Peseau

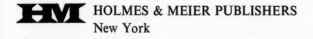
HOLMES & MEIER PUBLISHERS
New York

Published in the United States of America 1975 by
HOLMES & MEIER PUBLISHERS, INC
101 Fifth Avenue
New York, N.Y. 10003

Printed in Great Britain

Library of Congress Cataloging in Publication Data

Smyth, David J.
      Size, growth, profits, and executive compensation in the
large corporation.

      Bibliography: p.
      Includes index.
      1. Industries, Size of.   2. Profit.   3. Executives –
Salaries, pensions, etc.   4. Corporations – United States.
5. Corporations – Great Britain.   I. Boyes, William J.,
joint author.   II. Peseau, Dennis E., joint author.
III. Title.
HD69.S5S58   1975   338.6′44   74-34496
ISBN 0-8419-0198-8

Contents

List of Tables

Preface

This study was aided by a grant from the Research Committee of the Claremont Graduate School. We have also benefited from the co-operation of the Security Pacific National Bank, Los Angeles, and the Economics Division of the Southern California Edison Company, Rosemead, California.

Earlier versions of some of the chapters were presented at the annual meetings of the Econometric Society and the Western Economic Association and at seminars at various universities in the United Kingdom and the United States. We are indebted to the participants at these meetings and seminars for many helpful suggestions.

We are also indebted to Mrs Mary Gammons for typing numerous versions of the manuscript.

D.J.S.
W.J.B.
D.E.P.

1 Introduction

The object of this book is to examine some interrelationships between size, growth, profitability and executive compensation across large U.K. and U.S. corporations.

Our attention is restricted to large corporations and, for the most part, to industrial corporations, for four reasons. First, large corporations account for a major proportion of economic activity in the U.K. and U.S. economies – for instance, in 1972, 65 per cent of the sales, 75 per cent of the employment and 75 per cent of the profits of all U.S. industrial corporations were accounted for by the largest 500 firms. Secondly, limitation of the study to large firms makes the group of firms studied much more homogeneous than if we attempted to deal with smaller firms in the same analysis. Thirdly, the business and financial community devotes especial attention to the behaviour of the 500 largest industrial companies. Finally, data on a consistent basis are available for this sample of firms in both the United Kingdom and the United States.

Four major topics are dealt with in the present study: first, the relationship between alternative measures of firm size and between alternative measures of industrial concentration (Chapters 2 and 3, the first half of Chapter 4 and Chapter 5); secondly, the relationship between the rate of growth of firms and firm size (the second half of Chapter 4); thirdly, the behaviour of firm profitability (Chapters 6 and 7); and fourthly, the determinants of executive compensation (Chapters 8 and 9).

Sales, assets, employment and equity have been popular measures of firm size in empirical studies. We derive the conditions under which the results obtained from empirical studies will be independent of the specific measure of firm size used and find that the necessary conditions are not fulfilled for large U.K. and U.S. firms. Some implications of this finding for past and potential studies are pointed out. The problems involved in using alternative indices of industrial concentration are similar to those involved with alternative measures of firm size and again the necessary conditions under which the measures may be interchanged are not fulfilled.

The second half of Chapter 4 considers whether the rates at which firms grow are independent of their size. The finding is that in both the United Kingdom and the United States the smaller of the largest 500 firms grow faster than the larger of these firms.

Chapters 6 and 7 deal with the relationship between profitability and industrial concentration and report an examination of the time variability and inter-firm variability of profit rates in the United Kingdom and the United States. We find that the relationship between profitability and size depends on the measures of profitability and size used, that profitability is not correlated with concentration and that profit variability is not related to either size or concentration.

Much of the work on the theory of the firm assumes that firms are profit maximisers. This may be an unrealistic assumption for large management-controlled corporations and in Chapter 8, in an effort to ascertain the goals of the managers of large corporations, we examine whether U.S. executives are rewarded in accordance with profits or sales. We find both profits and sales to be important, there being a trade-off between the two. Chapter 9 finds that, for rate of return regulated firms, sales is the dominant variable.

Chapter 10 summarises the results obtained and presents our conclusions.

2 Alternative Measures of Firm Size: Some Theoretical Considerations

I INTRODUCTION

Much of the empirical work in industrial economics and in micro-economics involves the use of measures of firm size. Measures often adopted are sales, total assets, net assets, equity and employment. At times theoretical considerations make it clear which measure is appropriate but the measure may not be available. For instance, prior to the Companies Act of 1967, U.K. companies were not obliged to publish sales figures and most of them did not. Thus any researcher wishing to undertake empirical work using sales as his measure of firm size was faced with the problem that his sample size would be much smaller than if he used a more readily available measure such as net assets. Further, if he used sales his sample was likely to be a biased one, for in any year, one might expect the more successful companies to be the ones to publish sales. Consequently researchers have tended to use whichever measure of firm size was conveniently available. For this there were thought to be two justifications. First, that it was often not clear which measure was most desirable on theoretical grounds. Secondly, following Hart and Prais (1956) and Bates (1965), it was known that alternative measures of firm size were highly correlated and it was thought that this provided a sufficient condition for the interchangeability of alternative measures, i.e. that results obtained would be independent of the particular measure of firm size used.* It is in this sense that we use 'interchangeability' in this book. We shall demonstrate that, for alternative measures of firm size to be interchangeable, more rigorous

* Studies that used this justification included some by one of the present authors – Samuels and Smyth (1968, p. 128) and Smyth, Samuels and Tzoannos (1972, p. 78).

conditions are necessary than is provided by high correlations between the measures.

Essentially firm size enters into empirical studies in two ways. First, the researcher may desire to estimate the magnitude of response of some variable to firm size. For example, the dependent variable may be profits as in the studies by Benishay (1961), Hall and Weiss (1967), Marcus (1969), Eatwell (1971), Gale (1972), Kamerschen (1968), Radice (1971), Samuels and Smyth (1968) and Singh and Whittington (1968), innovative activity as in Horowitz (1962), Scherer (1965a and b), Smyth, Samuels and Tzoannos (1972) and Mansfield (1963, 1964), money and liquid-asset holdings as in Meltzer (1963), Maddala and Vogel (1965), Vogel and Maddala (1967) and De Allessi (1966), or productivity as in Griliches (1967b) and Fleming (1970).

Many studies utilise firm-size data in a different way – they are concerned with the relative growth rates of firms of different size, asking the question 'Is a firm's rate of growth independent of its size?' Such studies are concerned with the size distribution of firms and with comparisons between the size of firms at two different points of time; they include Aislabie (1971), Armstrong and Silbertson (1965), Eatwell (1971), Gibrat (1957), George (1964), Hart (1962) (1965, 1968), Hymer and Pashigian (1962), Mansfield (1962), Rowthorn (1971), Samuels (1965), Silberman (1967) and Singh and Whittington (1968).

The conditions under which alternative measures of firm size may be interchanged, i.e. results are independent of the measure of firm size used, differ according to the purpose for which the measures are to be used. In the present chapter, we shall derive the conditions under which the measures may be interchanged for those studies relating some variable to firm size, and relevant empirical evidence will be presented in Chapter 3. In Chapter 4 on size and growth of firms, the conditions for interchangeability required there will be derived together with some empirical evidence.

2 CONDITIONS UNDER WHICH EMPIRICAL RESULTS ARE INDEPENDENT OF THE MEASURE OF FIRM SIZE

Consider two alternative measures of firm size, X_1 and X_2. Suppose that these are perfectly correlated and all observations fall along the straight line

$$X_1 = a + bX_2 \tag{2.1}$$

It does not follow that the two measures may be used interchangeably. Suppose that we are interested in whether a variable Y increases more or less than proportionately with firm size X_2 where X_2 is the measure of firm size suggested by theoretical considerations but X_1 is used instead. We then fit

$$Y = g + hX_1 \tag{2.2}$$

and find that g is negative and h is positive and conclude that Y increases more than proportionately with firm size since the marginal relationship between Y and X_1 is constant and the average relationship, Y/X_1, is rising as X_1 is increased.

Substituting for X_1 from (2.1) in (2.2) yields

$$Y = (g + ah) + bhX_2 \tag{2.3}$$

If a is positive then ah is positive and, as g is negative, the sign of the constant term in (2.3), $g + ah$, is uncertain; it can be positive, negative or zero. The sign of bh is positive as both b and h are positive. If $c + ah$ is positive then variable Y increases less than proportionately than firm size measured by X_2 whereas it increases more than proportionately than firm size measured by X_1 even though X_1 and X_2 are perfectly correlated. Clearly if $a = 0$ and the measures are proportional to each other this problem does not arise.

We may consider the same effect in terms of a logarithmic model. We prefer such a model for two reasons. First, as we shall see in the next section, widely used measures of firm size may be regarded as inputs or outputs in firms' production functions, and typically the production functions used – such as the Cobb–Douglas production function – are multiplicative and hence linear in the logarithms. Secondly, because of the enormous variation in the absolute size of firms, however measured, even if consideration is limited to the largest 500 companies, residual errors are likely to demonstrate extreme heteroscedasticity; we shall see in Chapter 3 that the use of logarithms removes the heteroscedasticity.

Consider now perfect correlation between the natural logarithms of the two alternative measures of firm size so that

$$X_1 = AX_2^\beta \tag{2.4}$$

where both A and β are positive. Denoting natural logarithms by lower-case letters, so that $x_1 = \ln X_1$ and $x_2 = \ln X_2$, and writing $\alpha = \ln A$, we have

$$x_1 = \alpha + \beta x_2 \qquad (2.5)$$

where both α and β are positive. X_1 increases less than proportionately proportionately, or more than proportionately to X_2 according to whether β is less than, equal to, or greater than one. β is the elasticity of X_1 with respect to X_2, for the elasticity is given by

$$\frac{dX_1}{dX_2} \cdot \frac{X_2}{X_1} = \frac{A\beta X_2^{\beta-1} \cdot X_2}{X_1} = \frac{A\beta X_2^{\beta}}{A X_2^{\beta}} = \beta \qquad (2.6)$$

If we fit

$$y = \gamma + \delta x_1 \qquad (2.7)$$

which implies

$$Y = \Gamma X_1^{\delta} \qquad (2.8)$$

where $\gamma = \ln \Gamma$ and $y = \ln Y$ then we conclude that Y increases less than proportionately, proportionately, or more than proportionately to firm size measured by X_1 according to whether δ is less than, equal to, or greater than one. However, substituting for X_1 and x_1 from (2.4) and (2.5) in (2.8) and (2.7) respectively gives

$$Y = \Gamma A^{\delta} X_2^{\beta\delta} \qquad (2.9)$$

and

$$y = \gamma + \delta\alpha + \beta\delta x_2 \qquad (2.10)$$

According to the measure of firm size X_2, from (2.10), Y increases less than proportionately, proportionately, or more than proportionately to firm size if $\beta\delta$ is less than, equal to, or greater than one. It is clear that the alternative measures of firm size will yield the same elasticity for Y with respect to firm size only if $\beta\delta = \delta$ which requires that $\beta = 1$ (for non-zero δ) so that

$$X_1 = A X_2 \qquad (2.11)$$

and

$$x_1 = \alpha + x_2 \qquad (2.12)$$

The condition that $\beta = 1$ means that X_1 and X_2 must be proportional to each other if the results obtained are to be independent of the measure of firm size used.

We have shown that irrespective of whether alternative measures of firm size are perfectly correlated in their actual values or in their logarithms the measures may only be interchanged under the restrictive condition that the measures are proportional to each other.

3 ALTERNATIVE MEASURES OF FIRM SIZE

Is the condition under which alternative measures of firms may be interchanged likely to be a difficult one to fulfil? Can we demonstrate proportionality between the measures?

Let us consider these questions in terms of the theory of the firm. Measures of firm size that are found in the literature consist of three types: first, inputs into the productive process; secondly outputs; thirdly, measures of the value of a firm.

In the first category, we have the number of employees of a firm, the labour input, and some measure of assets representing the capital input. Employment is used in Armstrong and Silbertson (1965), Ferguson (1960), Fleming (1970), Griliches (1967b), Horowitz (1962), Scherer (1965a) and Steindl (1945). Assets are used in Aislabie (1971), Barna (1962), Cohen and Smyth (1973), Davenport (1971), Ferguson (1960), Hall and Weiss (1967), Hart (1965, 1968), Larner (1966), Mackintosh (1963), Marcus (1969), Marris (1971), Mermelstein (1969), Radice (1971), Samuels and Smyth (1965), Singh and Whittington (1968) and Smyth, Samuels and Tzoannos (1972).

Physical output is rarely used as a measure of firm size except where physical measures are meaningful, as in the oil industry. Instead a monetary value such as sales is widely used in the United States and is likely to be increasingly used in the United Kingdom since the 1967 Companies Act made the publication of sales figures mandatory.* Sales is the measure of firm size used to rank firms in our basic sources – *Fortune 500* and *The Times 1000* – and is the measure adopted in Diwan (1970), Ferguson (1960), Gale (1973,) Kamerschen (1968), Rowthorn (1971), Scherer (1965a) (1965b) and Whalen (1965).

Finally, we have as a measure of firm size some indicator of the value of the firm, stockholders' equity. Equity is used in Benishay (1961), De Alessi (1966), Florence (1957), Hart and Prais (1956), Hart (1962) and Kamerschen (1968).

---

* Sales differ from the monetary value of output to the extent that there are changes in the stock of inventories.

Profits have been used as a firm-size measure by Hart (1965, 1968). We do not regard profits as a satisfactory measure of firm size (for instance, profits may be negative) and we shall not consider it as such. Rather we regard profits as a variable to be related to firm size – see Chapters 6 and 7.

Consider now the production function

$$X_S = \varphi[X_E, X_A] \tag{2.13}$$

where X_S, X_E, X_A denote sales (= output if there is no change in stocks), employment and assets respectively. The inputs X_E and X_A will be proportional only if the expansion path in an isoquant diagram is a straight line through the origin. Production functions are divided into categories according to the properties they prescribe onto the isoquant surfaces and hence on the resulting expansion paths. The class of functions termed homothetic, where if each input is increased by some proportion, r, then output is increased by some function of r, i.e.

$$\varphi(r)X_S = \varphi[X_E.r, X_A.r] \tag{2.14}$$

produce parallel isoquants and hence linear expansion paths. The most commonly used of such functions is the Cobb–Douglas function. However, the property of homotheticity is not one that can be applied or assumed *a priori*, rather this property must be tested for since there are many useful functions such as the generalised CES function, the CRES function, for which the property of homotheticity does not hold.

Even if, for a particular industry, one could expect proportionality between inputs, i.e. a homothetic function, one could not expect the same function to be applicable across industries. Hence in a cross-section of industries the proportionality requirements would not be met overall even if they were met for individual industries, as capital–labour ratios differ between industries. Griliches (1967a, 1967b, 1968) found the hypothesis that distribution, efficiency and scale parameters are the same for all 2-digit industries inconsistent with the evidence. Walters (1963) considers many other examples.

Consider now the relationship between output and inputs in the production function. Even if the expansion path is a straight line through the origin, output will be proportional to inputs only if there are constant returns to scale. There is considerable evidence suggesting that constant returns to scale is not the rule in the U.K.

and U.S. economies – for instance Walters (1963), Dhrymes (1965) and Eisner and Nadiri (1968).

Finally, we consider the relationship between the value of a firm and its inputs and outputs. One might expect at least assets and value of the firm to be proportional, for if assets double, one might expect investors to demand that on average profits be doubled and hence the value of the firm be doubled. However, this suggests that large and small firms are equally adept at utilising assets so that profits are proportional to assets and therefore that the average profit flow is the only variable that enters into the utility functions of investors. We shall examine the relationship between firm size and profitability in Chapters 6 and 7 and we know that the variance of rates of return, and higher moments as well, may enter into the preference functions of investors – see for instance Markowitz (1959) and Samuelson (1970). Thus the stock market may not be neutral with respect to firm size.

The examination of theoretical considerations makes it clear that we cannot be sure *a priori* that different measures of firm size will be proportional to each other – rather there are good reasons why they should not be proportional. How alternative measures of firm size are related to each other is then an empirical question, and it is to a consideration of the empirical evidence that we now turn.

3 Alternative Measures of Firm Size: Empirical Evidence

1 INTRODUCTION: THE DATA

We now present empirical evidence on how some different measures of firm size are related. Our data are for the 1000 largest U.K. industrial corporations as given in the annual issues of *The Times 1000 Leading Companies in Britain and Overseas*, and for the 500 largest U.S. industrial corporations as given in the annual issues of *Fortune's Directory of the Largest 500 Corporations*. The size measures are sales, assets, employment and equity in both countries. For the United Kingdom the assets measure is net assets, for the United States it is total assets. The samples are chosen on the basis of sales in both countries. In both countries the coverage is limited to industrial corporations. For the United Kingdom, the nationalised industries, banks, finance houses, property companies, accepting houses, insurance companies, unit trusts, investment trusts and mining-finance companies are excluded. For the United States, commercial banking companies, life-insurance companies, diversified financial companies, retailing companies, transport companies and utilities are excluded. The coverage in the two countries seems to be similar except that retailing companies are included for the United Kingdom but not for the United States.

2 DEFINITIONS OF THE UNITED KINGDOM AND UNITED STATES FIRM-SIZE MEASURES

The alternative measures of firm size are defined as follows.

United Kingdom
  Sales = turnover.

Net assets = capital employed, defined as total tangible assets less current liabilities and sundry provisions (other than bank loans and overdrafts and future tax).

Employment = total number of employees.

Equity = market value of equity, the number of shares outstanding multiplied by the price of the share on 21 July.

United States

Sales = net sales defined as gross sales and other operating revenue less discounts, returns and allowances. Included are service and rental revenues but all companies on the list must have derived more than 50 per cent of their revenues from manufacturing and/or mining. Sales of subsidiaries are included when they are consolidated; sales from discontinued operations are included when these figures are published. Sales figures do not include excise taxes collected by the manufacturer and so the figures for some corporations may be lower than those published by the corporations themselves.

Assets = total assets employed in the business at the company's year end less depreciation and depletion. It represents current assets plus net plant plus other non-current assets (including intangible assets and deferred items).

Employment = the number of company workers.

Equity = stockholders' equity or invested capital, defined as the sum of capital stock, surplus and retained earnings at year end. It represents common stock plus retained earnings, capital surplus, self-insurance reserves, unamortised-debt premium, capital stock premium less common treasury stock, intangibles, accumulated unpaid preferred dividend, excess of involuntary liquidating value of outstanding preferred stock over carrying value and deferred taxes and investment credit.

3 STATISTICAL CONSIDERATIONS

We must now choose the form in which we shall examine the empirical relationship between alternative measures of firm size; whether we shall fit relationships that are linear in the actual values, as in equation (2.1), or whether we fit relationships linear in the logarithms as in equation (2.5). It will be recalled that the theoretical implications of the two specifications are the same but one may be preferable from a statistical point of view.

The models in Chapter 2 have been presented in purely determin-istic terms – in order to simplify the presentation no stochastic terms were included. It is now necessary to specify stochastic terms. The conventional and simplest procedure is to specify that the errors are distributed normally for the actual-values model – equation (2.1) – and log-normally for the linear in logarithms model – equation (2.5). We expect the second assumption to be more satisfactory as in actual values there are enormous differences in the size of firms, however measured. For instance, for the United Kingdom in 1972-3 the sales of the largest firm, British Petroleum, are £3153 million while those for the 500th firm, Crittall-Hope Engineering, are £21.5 million, the ratio of these sales being 146.4 to 1. Similarly for the United States in 1971 the sales of the largest firm, General Motors, are $28,264 million and those for the 500th firm, Hanes, are $176.1 million, a ratio of 160.5 to 1. On the other hand the ratios of the natural logarithms of the sales of the largest and 500th firms in the United Kingdom and the United States respectively are only 1.30 and 1.27. We thus expect the disturbance terms in the actual-values model to be heteroscedastic.

Heteroscedasticity arises when the variance of the error term differs among various observations, i.e. the variance is not constant. In the present case, we expect the variance of the error term to be positively correlated with firm size. If heteroscedasticity is present then while parameter estimates will be unbiased and consistent the standard errors of estimated regression coefficients will tend to be under-estimated. In the present context, this means that we might un-warrantedly reject the null hypothesis of proportionality between alternative measures of firm size.

We ran regressions for both the linear in actual values model and the linear in logarithms model (for reasons indicated below, ortho-gonal regressions were fitted); we then tested to see if heteroscedasti-city was present in the residuals. The test used is described in Gold-feld and Quandt (1965) and Glejser (1969). We ranked the firms by size and divided the sample into two. Regressions were then fitted to the two subgroups and the ratio of the sum of the squared errors for the two subgroups was calculated. If we assume that the error terms are normally distributed then the ratio of the sum of the squared errors is the ratio of two independent chi-square distributions, i.e. an F-ratio, with $[(n/2) - 1, (n/2) - 1]$ degrees of freedom, where n is the number of observations in the complete sample. We then tested to see if the F-ratios were significantly different from unity. For the model involving actual values, homoscedasticity was rejected at the 1 per cent level for all pairs, the variance of the error terms increasing with firm size. However, when the logarithmic model was used the null hypothesis of homoscedasticity was accepted at the 10 per cent level for all pairs and at the 5 per cent level for many pairs. We thus regard the logarithmic specification as the more satisfactory one statistically and we shall only report the results for this specification.*

A second statistical problem is that, in comparing any two measures of firm size, there is no justification for assigning one measure as a random variable and the other measure as fixed or distributed independently of the disturbance term. We wish to estimate β in the relation

$$x_1 = \alpha + \beta x_2 \qquad (3.1)$$

and test to see if it is significantly different from unity. If we apply ordinary least-squares (OLS) regression analysis we may either fit

$$x_1 = \alpha_1 + \beta_1 x_2 + \varepsilon_1 \qquad (3.2)$$

or

$$x_2 = \alpha_2 + \beta_2 x_1 + \varepsilon_2 \qquad (3.3)$$

where x_1 and x_2 are the logarithms of the alternative measures of firm size X_1 and X_2 and ε_1 and ε_2 are error terms. We may thus estimate β either from $\beta = \beta_1$ or from $\beta = 1/\beta_2$. The ordinary least-squares regression procedure estimates a regression line by minimising the sum of squares in a direction perpendicular to the variable denoted as the dependent variable. Thus we may estimate either

$$\beta = \beta_1 = m_{12}/m_{22} \qquad (3.4)$$

or

$$\beta = 1/\beta_2 = m_{11}/m_{12} \qquad (3.5)$$

where the ms denote moments about the mean.† These estimates of

---

* We are aware that the assumption of normality for the error terms for the actual-values model cannot be made simultaneously with the assumption of normality for the logarithmic model. However, even without the normality assumption, the test gives a good indication of the presence or absence of heteroscedasticity. See Scheffé (1959, Chapter 10) for a detailed discussion of the sensitivity of F-tests under violations of the normality assumption.

† Denoting the respective means of x_1 and x_2 by $\bar{x}_1$ and $\bar{x}_2$, we have $m_{11} = \Sigma(x_1 - \bar{x}_1)^2$, $m_{22} = \Sigma(x_2 - \bar{x}_2)^2$ and $m_{12} = \Sigma(x_1 - \bar{x}_1)(x_2 - \bar{x}_2)$.

β will only be the same if

$$\frac{m_{12}}{m_{22}} = \frac{m_{11}}{m_{12}} \qquad (3.6)$$

that is,

$$\frac{m_{12}^2}{m_{11}m_{22}} = 1 \qquad (3.7)$$

The left-hand side of (3.6) is r^2, the square of the correlation coefficient between x_1 and x_2. Thus the two ordinary least-squares regressions (3.4) and (3.5) will yield identical estimates of β only if x_1 and x_2 are perfectly correlated. Our empirical analysis indicates that this is not the case and there are marked differences in the value of β depending on whether it is estimated by $\beta = \beta_1$ or $\beta = 1/\beta_2$.

To cope with this problem, we compute orthogonal regressions which minimise the sum of the squares of the errors perpendicular to the regression line.* We thus estimate β by

$$\hat{\beta} = \frac{2m_{12}}{m_{11} - m_{22} + \sqrt{\{(m_{11} - m_{22})^2 + 4m_{12}^2\}}} \qquad (3.8)$$

The orthogonal regression coefficient is bounded by the estimates β_1 and $1/\beta_2$; it is thus a compromise between the two natural regressions and provides a more reliable estimate of the true elasticity between the measures.

4 EMPIRICAL EVIDENCE FOR THE UNITED KINGDOM

We undertook ordinary least-squares regression analysis and orthogonal regression analysis for the 500 largest U.K. firms for the years 1970–71, 1971–2 and 1972–3. Also for the year 1971–2 we repeated the analysis for the 1000 largest firms.

Some gaps exist in the data. Equity estimates are available only for quoted companies, and employment estimates are unavailable for some firms. Sales and assets figures are available for all firms. As we used the maximum number of observations that are available in each regression the number of observations varies from regression to regression. Table 3.1 gives the number of firms out of the largest 500 that could be included in each pair of measures for 1971–2 – the

---

* See Goldberger (1968), Linnick (1961) and Malinvaud (1966) for discussions of orthogonal regression techniques.

figures for the other years are similar – and Table 3.2 gives the numbers for the full 1000.

Tables 3.3 to 3.6 give the ordinary least-squares results. In each cell of these tables the first coefficient gives the estimate of β obtained

TABLE 3.1

Number of observations in United Kingdom regressions: 500 largest industrial corporations, 1971–2

	Assets	Employment	Equity
Sales	500	485	389
Assets		485	389
Employment			379

TABLE 3.2

Number of observations in United Kingdom regressions: 1000 largest industrial corporations, 1971–2

	Assets	Employment	Equity
Sales	1000	966	758
Assets		966	758
Employment			756

TABLE 3.3

OLS estimates: United Kingdom, 1970–71, 500 largest industrial corporations

	Assets	Employment	Equity
Sales	0.621	0.517	0.501
	0.939	1.258	0.904
	0.661	0.411	0.554
Assets		0.829	0.775
		1.305	1.022
		0.635	0.758
Employment			0.623
			1.154
			0.540

Note: In each cell the first row is the estimate of $\beta = \beta_1$; the second row is the estimate of $\beta = 1/\beta_2$ where β is the elasticity of the measure on the left to the measure listed above; the third row gives the estimated r^2.

by regressing x_1 on x_2 (i.e. β_1), and the second coefficient is the estimate of β obtained by regressing x_2 on x_1 (i.e. $1/\beta_2$); the final coefficient is the coefficient of determination, r^2. That the correlations are far from perfect and that (3.4) and (3.5) yield markedly different estimates of β is apparent from the tables.

TABLE 3.4

OLS estimates: United Kingdom, 1971–2,
500 largest industrial corporations

	Assets	Employment	Equity
Sales	0.631	0.532	0.492
	1.035	1.299	0.893
	0.653	0.410	0.551
Assets		0.891	0.754
		1.385	1.020
		0.643	0.739
Employment			0.614
			1.181
			0.520

Note: See Table 3.3.

TABLE 3.5

OLS estimates: United Kingdom, 1971–2,
1000 largest industrial corporations

	Assets	Employment	Equity
Sales	0.649	0.604	0.579
	1.013	1.201	1.001
	0.641	0.503	0.578
Assets		0.829	0.776
		1.281	1.042
		0.647	0.744
Employment			0.632
			1.121
			0.564

Note: See Table 3.3.

Tables 3.7 to 3.10 report the orthogonal regression results. Successive rows in each cell give the elasticity of the measure listed on the left to the measure listed above, the standard error and the t-value calculated with respect to an elasticity of unity. The elasticity of the measure listed above to the measure listed on the left may be obtained by taking the reciprocal of the first row of the appropriate

TABLE 3.6

OLS estimates: United Kingdom, 1972–3
500 largest industrial corporations

	Assets	Employment	Equity
	0.666	0.557	0.540
Sales	0.933	1.157	0.939
	0.714	0.481	0.575
		0.839	0.792
Assets		1.319	1.076
		0.636	0.736
			0.650
Employment			1.182
			0.550

Note: See Table 3.3.

TABLE 3.7

Orthogonal regression estimates: United Kingdom, 1970–71, 500 largest industrial corporations

	Assets	Employment	Equity
	0.713	0.699	0.594
Sales	0.026	0.042	0.027
	10.98	7.14	15.04
		1.069	0.875
Assets		0.044	0.025
		1.56	5.00
			0.800
Employment			0.038
			5.26

Note: In each cell the first row is the orthogonal regression coefficient indicating the elasticity of the measure listed on the left to the measure listed above; the second row is the standard error; the third row is the t-statistic calculated with respect to an elasticity of unity. The elasticity of the measure listed above to the measure listed on the left may be obtained by taking the reciprocal of the first row of the appropriate cell.

cell. The hypothesis of proportionality between a pair of measures is rejected if the t-value given is significant. In each of the tables, we have six pairs of measures. The results are surprisingly consistent. All the coefficients in all four tables are significantly different from unity at the 1 per cent level except those between assets and employment in all tables. Accordingly the results present very strong evidence against the null hypothesis of proportionality. Hence conclusions from empirical studies will not be independent of size measures used.

TABLE 3.8

Orthogonal regression estimates: United Kingdom
1971–2, 500 largest industrial corporations

	Assets	Employment	Equity
Sales	0.753	0.682	0.677
	0.023	0.041	0.031
	10.63	7.77	10.42
Assets		1.112	0.859
		0.069	0.026
		1.62	5.42
Employment			0.801
			0.040
			4.98

Note: See Table 3.7.

TABLE 3.9

Orthogonal regression estimates: United Kingdom
1971–2, 1000 largest industrial corporations

	Assets	Employment	Equity
Sales	0.781	0.784	0.761
	0.018	0.027	0.024
	12.20	8.01	9.92
Assets		1.041	0.872
		0.026	0.019
		1.59	6.62
Employment			0.784
			0.025
			8.50

Note: See Table 3.7.

The elasticity of sales with respect to the other three measures is always less than one. This is a particularly important finding because sales is a measure that is often used in empirical studies in the United States and would have been used in U.K. studies had it been available.

TABLE 3.10

Orthogonal regression estimates: United Kingdom, 1972–3, 500 largest industrial corporations

	Assets	Employment	Equity
Sales	0.745	0.732	0.678
	0.026	0.042	0.031
	9.98	6.31	10.39
Assets		1.041	0.911
		0.033	0.029
		1.23	3.07
Employment			0.836
			0.040
			4.07

Note: See Table 3.7.

The elasticity of assets with respect to sales is greater than one, that with respect to equity is less than one, and that with respect to employment is not significantly different from one. Employment elasticity with respect to sales is greater than one, with respect to equity it is less than one.

The elasticity of equity with respect to the other three measures is greater than one. This suggests that the stock market favours large firms (as measured by sales, assets or employment) to smaller firms. We shall have to wait until Chapters 6 and 7 to see if this is warranted by these larger firms being relatively more attractive through the behaviour of their profits.

5 EMPIRICAL EVIDENCE FOR THE UNITED STATES

We undertake an analysis of alternative measures of firm size for the 500 largest industrial companies for five years – 1963, 1965, 1968, 1970 and 1972. These years cover all stages of the cycle, 1970 being a recession year.

Tables 3.11 to 3.15 give the ordinary least-squares results. As for the United Kingdom, the correlations are not high enough to prevent substantial differences in the estimates of β from $β_1$ and $1/β_2$.

Tables 3.16 to 3.20 report the orthogonal regression results. Again the results are surprisingly consistent. All the elasticities are significantly different from one at the 1 per cent level except that the sales–employment elasticity for 1965 is only significant at the 5 per cent

TABLE 3.11

OLS estimates: United States, 1963, 500 largest industrial corporations

	Assets	Employment	Equity
Sales	0.790	0.807	0.732
	0.979	1.093	0.987
	0.807	0.738	0.742
Assets		0.857	0.937
		1.333	0.997
		0.643	0.940
Employment			0.692
			1.181
			0.586

Note: In each cell the first row is the estimate of β = $β_1$; the second row is the estimate of β = $1/β_2$ where β is the elasticity of the measure on the left to the measure listed above; the third row gives the estimated r^2.

TABLE 3.12

OLS estimates: United States, 1965, 500 largest industrial corporations

	Assets	Employment	Equity
Sales	0.803	0.813	0.734
	0.982	1.121	0.992
	0.817	0.725	0.740
Assets		0.856	0.925
		1.353	1.000
		0.633	0.925
Employment			0.679
			1.175
			0.578

Note: See Table 3.11.

level and the assets–employment coefficients are not significant at even the 10 per cent level except for 1963 and 1965. The elasticity of assets with respect to employment is less than one in 1970 and non-significant and greater than one in all other years; apart from this no elasticities switch from being less than or greater than one in any two years so the results are very stable. We conclude that researchers' conclusions will depend on the measure of firm size used for five of the six pairs, the exception being assets–employment.

TABLE 3.13

OLS estimates: United States, 1968,
500 largest industrial corporations

	Assets	Employment	Equity
Sales	0.801	0.804	0.743
	0.978	1.100	0.989
	0.819	0.731	0.751
Assets		0.839	0.930
		1.346	0.991
		0.623	0.938
Employment			0.658
			1.193
			0.552

Note: See Table 3.11.

TABLE 3.14

OLS estimates: United States, 1970,
500 largest industrial corporations

	Assets	Employment	Equity
Sales	0.781	0.683	0.560
	0.939	1.030	0.951
	0.832	0.663	0.578
Assets		0.776	0.696
		1.232	1.008
		0.629	0.690
Employment			0.772
			1.778
			0.434

Note: See Table 3.11.

TABLE 3.15

OLS estimates: United States, 1972,
500 largest industrial corporations

	Assets	Employment	Equity
Sales	0.781	0.773	0.724
	1.051	1.036	1.037
	0.823	0.801	0.752
Assets		0.671	0.936
		1.277	0.993
		0.857	0.929
Employment			0.692
			0.884
			0.612

Note: See Table 3.11.

TABLE 3.16

Orthogonal regression estimates: United States,
1963, 500 largest industrial corporations

	Assets	Employment	Equity
Sales	0.866	0.929	0.827
	0.019	0.025	0.022
	7.05	2.84	7.86
Assets		1.086	0.965
		0.036	0.011
		2.39	3.18
Equity			0.877
			0.033
			3.72

Note: In each cell the first row is the orthogonal regression coefficient indicating the elasticity of the measure listed on the left to the measure listed above; the second row is the standard error; the third row is the t-statistic calculated with respect to an elasticity of unity. The elasticity of the measure listed above to the measure listed on the left may be obtained by taking the reciprocal of the first row of the appropriate cell.

TABLE 3.17

Orthogonal regression estimates: United States, 1965, 500 largest industrial corporations

	Assets	Employment	Equity
Sales	0.877 0.019 6.63	0.947 0.026 2.02	0.832 0.022 7.61
Assets		1.096 0.038 2.57	0.960 0.012 3.27
Equity			0.862 0.033 4.16

Note: See Table 3.16.

TABLE 3.18

Orthogonal regression estimates: United States, 1968, 500 largest industrial corporations

	Assets	Employment	Equity
Sales	0.833 0.018 9.51	0.924 0.025 2.97	0.822 0.021 8.63
Assets		1.050 0.037 1.36	0.957 0.011 4.05
Employment			0.871 0.034 3.766

Note: See Table 3.16.

TABLE 3.19

Orthogonal regression estimates: United States, 1970, 500 largest industrial corporations

	Assets	Employment	Equity
Sales	0.851	0.813	0.649
	0.017	0.023	0.022
	8.82	8.26	18.91
Assets		0.981	0.809
		0.028	0.022
		0.72	8.63
Employment			0.789
			0.041
			5.12

Note: See Table 3.16.

TABLE 3.20

Orthogonal regression estimates: United States, 1972, 500 largest industrial corporations

	Assets	Employment	Equity
Sales	0.847	0.914	0.813
	0.018	0.026	0.021
	8.50	3.25	8.91
Assets		1.071	0.939
		0.047	0.012
		1.52	5.08
Employment			0.881
			0.033
			3.64

Note: See Table 3.16.

It is remarkable how similar the U.S. and U.K. patterns are. Table 3.21 gives the average elasticities for the three years for the 500 largest U.K. corporations and for the five years for the 500 largest U.S. corporations. The only consistent difference between the results

TABLE 3.21

Comparison of average elasticities between alternative size measures: United Kingdom and United States

	Assets	Employment	Equity
Sales	0.749	0.722	0.677
	0.841	0.904	0.788
Assets		1.074	0.869
		1.057	0.926
Employment			0.795
			0.856

Note: In each cell the average elasticity for the measure on the left to the measure listed above is given for the United Kingdom in the first row (average of three years, 500 largest industrial corporations) and for the United States in the second row (average for five years, 500 largest industrial corporations).

for the two countries is that the elasticity for sales with respect to the other measures is larger in the United States. This is most marked for the sales–employment elasticity presumably reflecting U.S. corporations' greater efficiency in utilising factors of production, especially labour, as the rate of production increases.

6 SOME IMPLICATIONS OF THE RESULTS FOR PREVIOUS EMPIRICAL STUDIES

We now point out the implications of our results for some previous empirical work.

A number of U.K. studies have found that the rate of profit declines with firm size as measured by assets – Radice (1971), Samuels and Smyth (1968) and Singh and Whittington (1968). As size measured by sales increases more slowly than size measured by assets, it follows that profit rates decline faster with firm size if size is measured by sales than if size is measured by assets. Size measured by equity increases faster than size measured by assets so if firm size were measured by equity then the decline in profit rates with size would be less marked. We return to the relationship between profitability and firm size in the United Kingdom in Chapter 6.

In a study of money holdings of firms in the United Kingdom, De Alessi (1966) found the elasticity of the demand for money to be about unity. De Alessi used equity as his measure of firm size and we have found that the elasticity of equity with respect to the other three measures of firm size is greater than one. Thus if De Alessi had used one of the other measures of firm size, we should expect him to have concluded not that the demand for money is unit elastic with respect to firm size but that its elasticity is greater than one, i.e. that there are diseconomies of scale in holding money.

In his study of the money holdings of firms in the United States, Meltzer (1963) used sales as the measure of firm size and found the resulting elasticity of demand for money with respect to firm size to be unity or just slightly greater than unity. The elasticity of sales with respect to all the alternative measures are less than one; thus, had Meltzer used measures of firm size other than sales, he might have concluded not that the demand for money is unit elastic or larger but that there are economies of scale in money holdings.

A final example demonstrating the implications of our results is a study by Scherer (1965b) where he finds, using sales as the measure of firm size, that inventive inputs and patents increase less than proportionately with firm size. From our results it would seem that Scherer's conclusions would have been much stronger had assets or employment been used as the measure of firm size. However, as far as employment is concerned these conclusions are inconsistent with those derived by Scherer (1965a) in a companion study. In that study the inventive activity-to-sales relationship was found to lie between the inventive activity-to-assets and inventive activity-to-employment relationships, not uniformly on one side of them. One explanation of why our implied results differ is that Scherer's results or ours or both may be linear approximations to non-linear relationships, and depending on where on the non-linear relationships the observed points are grouped, biases may arise in estimating linear equations. Scherer found some evidence of non-linearities (between patenting and sales), and in Chapter 4, we find some evidence of non-linearity between our size measures.

7 CONCLUSIONS

We have demonstrated in this chapter that the conditions necessary for conclusions concerning the elasticity of firm size and some variable to be independent of the actual measure of firm size are not fulfilled for large U.K. and U.S. firms. And we pointed out some implications of these results for past studies. Our results make it clear that future studies using empirical measures of firm size should not arbitrarily choose whichever measure is conveniently available. If theoretical considerations suggest a measure then it should be used. If the researcher is uncertain as to what measure is appropriate then he should not just arbitrarily pick a single measure but he should repeat his analysis using alternative measures.

4 Size and Growth of Firms

I INTRODUCTION

A question of major importance in industrial organisation is whether the size of a firm has any influence on its growth rate – that is, do large firms grow faster relatively than small firms or vice versa? This topic is the subject of the present chapter.

The typical size distribution of firms is positively skewed with a few large firms and many small firms so that the size distribution of firms is clearly not normal – see Hart (1962). In practice this skewness can often be removed by plotting the frequencies against the logarithm of size, resulting in a curve approximating the normal curve so that the original distribution may be deemed log normal – see Adelman (1958) and Hart (1962).

A normal curve is generated when a large number of small independent random forces act on a variable in an additive manner and a log-normal curve can be generated if they act multiplicatively. In the present context, this means that the determinants of the growth of firms tend to change the size of firms by randomly distributed proportions. Some forces make for an increase in the size of the firm, some make for a decrease but all act randomly in the sense that there is no tendency to favour or disfavour firms of any particular size. Gibrat (1957) proposed a 'law of proportionate effect' which stated that the proportional change in the size of a firm is independent of its absolute size, in other words that large and small firms have the same average proportionate rates of growth. This is contrary to the idea that over time large firms are dominating an increasing share of the market, i.e. that concentration is increasing, which forms the basis for anti-trust and anti-monopoly legislation in the United States and the United Kingdom. Of course, it is also contrary to the idea that the size of firms tend to equalise over time or that some optimal firm size exists for combining inputs to produce outputs.

A number of studies have attempted to test the law of proportionate effect; these have included Aislabie (1971), Armstrong and Silbertson (1965), Eatwell (1971), Gibrat (1957), George (1964), Hart (1962, 1965, 1968), Hart and Prais (1956), Hymer and Pashigian (1962), Mansfield (1962), Rowthorn (1971), Samuels (1965) and Singh and Whittington (1968). The hypothesis is appealing for it implies a certain distribution of sizes of firms – see Aitchison and Brown (1963) for a discussion of the properties of the log-normal distribution.

Using the notation of Chapter 2 where X is firm size and x is its natural logarithm then proportionality of growth may be investigated by fitting

$$x(t + 1) = \mu + \lambda x(t) \tag{4.1}$$

where (t) and $(t + 1)$ denote successive time periods. Taking the derivative of $x(t + 1)$ with respect to $x(t)$ gives

$$dx(t + 1)/dx(t) = \lambda \tag{4.2}$$

If $\lambda = 1$ then the rate of growth of firms is independent of firm size; if $\lambda > 1$ then large firms grow faster than small firms; if $\lambda < 1$ then small firms grow faster than large firms.

We may examine the proportionality assumption by fitting equation (4.1) and testing to see if λ is significantly different from unity; a project we undertake later in this chapter. First, however, we investigate whether results obtained from investigating growth rates of firms of different size are independent of the choice of variable to measure size. In section 4.2, we shall find that the condition necessary for the measures to be interchangeable is weaker than that found for the problem studied in Chapters 2 and 3, but that the empirical evidence suggests that the conditions are still not fulfilled (section 4.3). In sections 4.4 and 4.5, we consider empirical evidence on growth rates of firms of different size for the United States and the United Kingdom and our conclusions are presented in section 4.6.

2 CONDITIONS UNDER WHICH CONCLUSIONS CONCERNING GROWTH RATES ARE INDEPENDENT OF THE MEASURE OF FIRM SIZE

We use the notation of Chapter 2 and denote two alternative measures of firm size by X_1 and X_2 and their natural logarithms by

x_1 and x_2 respectively. Writing equation (4.1) for the two measures, we have

$$x_1(t + 1) = \mu_1 + \lambda_1 x_1(t) \tag{4.3}$$

and

$$x_2(t + 1) = \mu_2 + \lambda_2 x_2(t) \tag{4.4}$$

Taking derivatives gives us

$$dx_1(t + 1)/dx_1(t) = \lambda_1 \tag{4.5}$$

$$dx_2(t + 1)/dx_2(t) = \lambda_2 \tag{4.6}$$

The two measures will yield the same conclusion about the rate of growth of firms of different size, i.e. will be interchangeable, if λ_1 and λ_2 are equal.

We first consider the possibility that the two measures are linear in their logarithms – this is the assumption made in Chapter 2. We have

$$x_1 = \alpha + \beta x_2 \tag{4.7}$$

and writing (4.7) for time periods (t) and $(t + 1)$ gives

$$x_1(t) = \alpha + \beta x_2(t) \tag{4.8}$$

and

$$x_1(t + 1) = \alpha + \beta x_2(t + 1) \tag{4.9}$$

Substituting for $x_1(t)$ and $x_1(t + 1)$ from (4.8) and (4.9) in (4.3) and rearranging gives

$$x_2(t + 1) = [\mu_1 + \alpha(\lambda_1 - 1)]/\beta + \lambda_1 x_2(t) \tag{4.10}$$

and hence

$$dx_2(t + 1)/dx_2(t) = \lambda_1 \tag{4.11}$$

Thus the rate of growth in terms of x_2 is the same as in terms of x_1, for λ_1 and λ_2 are equal. Note that for interchangeability, we do not require that $\beta = 1$, the condition that we derived in Chapter 2. Provided the measures are linked log linearly then our conclusion about relative rates of growth is independent of the measure used.*

Now consider the possibility that x_1 and x_2 are related non-linearly, as, for instance,

$$x_1 = \alpha + \beta' x_2{}^\xi \tag{4.12}$$

* From equations (4.3), (4.4) and (4.10) we have $\mu_2 = [\mu_1 + \alpha(\lambda_1 - 1)]/\beta$ so even with $\lambda_1 = \lambda_2 = 1$ and hence $\mu_2 = \mu_1/\beta$ the rates of growth given by different measures will not be the same unless the measures are proportional ($\beta = 1$) but this is irrelevant to the comparison of relative rates of growth.

Writing (4.12) for periods (t) and $(t + 1)$ and substituting for $x_1(t)$ and $x_1(t + 1)$ in (4.3) and rearranging gives

$$x_2(t + 1) = \{[\mu + \alpha(\lambda_1 - 1)]/\beta' + \lambda_1 x_2^\xi(t)\}^{\xi/\xi} \qquad (4.13)$$

Taking the derivative of $x_2(t + 1)$ with respect to $x_2(t)$ gives

$$\lambda_2 = dx_2(t + 1)/dx_2(t)$$
$$= \lambda_1 x_2^{(1-\xi)}(t + 1)/x_2^{(1-\xi)}(t) \qquad (4.14)$$

Thus $\lambda_1 = \lambda_2$ only if $x_2^{(1-\xi)}(t)/x_2^{(1-\xi)}(t + 1) = 1$ which is the case only if $x(t + 1) = x(t)$, i.e. no growth, or $\xi = 1$, the linear case considered above. If we assume that there is growth then we have

$$\lambda_1/\lambda_2 = x_2^{(1-\xi)}(t)/x_2^{(1-\xi)}(t + 1) \lesseqgtr 1 \text{ as } \xi \lesseqgtr 1 \qquad (4.15)$$

More complex forms may be obtained by adding further terms to equation (4.12). For instance, if

$$x_1 = \alpha + \beta'x_2^\xi + \beta''x_2^\eta \qquad (4.16)$$

we have

$$\lambda_1 = \lambda_2 \frac{\beta'\xi x_2^{(1-\xi)}(t) + \beta''\eta x_2^{(1-\eta)}(t)}{\beta'\xi x_2^{(1-\xi)}(t + 1) + \beta''\eta x_2^{(1-\eta)}(t + 1)} \qquad (4.17)$$

We have shown that if the relationship between alternative measures of firm size is non-linear in the logarithms then different measures of firm size will yield different conclusions about the proportional rates of growth of firms of different sizes. We now see whether empirical evidence supports non-linear or linear relationships.

3 LINEAR AND NON-LINEAR RELATIONSHIPS BETWEEN ALTERNATIVE FIRM-SIZE MEASURES: EMPIRICAL EVIDENCE FOR THE UNITED KINGDOM AND THE UNITED STATES

Our data for the investigation of possible non-linearities between measures of firm size are a subset of the data used in Chapter 3. We fit regressions using the 1971–2 data for the 1000 largest U.K. firms and the 1968 data for the 500 largest U.S. firms.

In seeking to determine if the relationships between measures of firm size are non-linear in their logarithms, we shall consider equation (4.12) which is merely one of many possible non-linear specifications. We want to know whether or not ξ is one, for if it is then we reject non-linearity. Unfortunately it is not possible to estimate ξ directly in a non-linear equation such as (4.12). Accordingly we undertake a search procedure in which we parametrically vary ξ over the range -3 to 10 by increments of 0.1 and inspect the mean-square errors obtained. All values of ξ yielding the lowest mean-square errors are in the range $\xi = 0$ to $\xi = 4$ and the behaviour of the mean-square errors as ξ is varied is well-behaved as single minima are obtained. As we wish to compare the mean-squared errors of the non-linear formulations with the linear case, we give the ratios of the mean-square errors for $\xi = 1$ to the lowest mean-square errors obtained for other values of θ in Tables 4.1 and 4.2. It is

TABLE 4.1

Radio of mean-square error for linear
model to lowest mean-square error:
United Kingdom

	Assets	Employment	Equity
Sales	1.24	1.67	1.09
Assets		1.19	1.08
Employment			1.07

TABLE 4.2

Ratio of mean-square error for linear
model to lowest mean-square error:
United States

	Assets	Employment	Equity
Sales	1.11	1.16	1.16
Assets		1.08	1.15
Employment			1.03

tempting to test these as F-ratios but this would be illegitimate as the mean-square errors that are calculated are not independent. Accordingly it is not very clear how important non-linearities are. In Table 4.1, for the United Kingdom, there is marked reduction in the mean-square error between sales and employment and some appreciable reduction for the sales–assets and assets–employment regressions. The regressions involving equity show the least evidence of non-linearity. For the United States the largest reductions in mean-squared errors are for the sales–employment, sales–equity and assets–equity regressions.*

4 SIZE AND GROWTH OF FIRMS: EMPIRICAL EVIDENCE FOR THE UNITED STATES

We now undertake an empirical analysis of the relationship between size and rate of growth of firms for the United States.

We first consider firms on the *Fortune 500* list in 1972 and analyse their growth rates for the periods 1971–2 and 1963–72. These firms did not have to be on the *Fortune* list for 1971 or 1963 since the data bank from which the data were extracted included those firms whether in the *Fortune* lists or not – the *Fortune* list merely gave us the list of firms. We did not consider births and deaths of firms but considered only those firms that existed over the whole period, 1971–2 or 1963–72 as the case may be. For each size measure, i, we regressed

$$x_i (1972) = \mu_i + \lambda_i x_i (1971) \qquad (4.18)$$

and

$$x_i (1972) = \mu_i + \lambda_i x_i (1963) \qquad (4.19)$$

The results are reported in Table 4.3 where, in each case, we give the estimated values of λ, the standard error and the t-statistic calculated with respect to 1 and the coefficient of determination, r^2.

For the 1972 on 1971 regressions the estimated values of λ are all less than 1. The difference between the λ coefficient for employment and 1 is highly significant, the t-statistic is 4.13, the coefficients of sales and assets are significant at the 10 per cent level but not at the 5 per cent level, the coefficient of equity is not significant at the 10 per cent level – throughout this section we apply two-tailed tests as we have no hypothesis about whether λ is greater or less than 1.

The results for growth over the 1963–72 period are much more dramatic. All the coefficients are less than unity, and the t-values are all over 10 so that they are highly significant. These results strongly suggest that small firms grow faster than large firms.

We must now try to reconcile these one-year and ten-year results. In terms of economic theory the time horizon has an important

---

* The possible non-linear relationships between sales and employment may reconcile our results in Chapter 3 with those of Scherer (1965a), as noted in section 3.6.

influence on the behaviour of fixed and variable factors. In the short run, fixed factors – by definition – would not change whereas the variable factors may do so; in the long run both fixed and variable factors may change. If we regard one year as short run and ten years as long run, then consider employment as the variable factor and assets as the fixed factor, the results are consistent with the variable factor adjusting in both the short and long run and the fixed factor adjusting only in the long run. This does not, however, provide an explanation of the short and long-run behaviour of sales and equity.

TABLE 4.3

Growth and firm size: regression results,
United States and United Kingdom

Size measure	Coefficients and statistics	United States			United Kingdom
		x (1972) over x (1971)	x (1972) over x (1963) Sample by 1972	Sample by 1963	x (1972–3) over x (1971–2)
Sales	λ	0.9904	0.7098	0.9290	0.9322
	Standard error	0.0057	0.021	0.023	0.0108
	t-statistic w.r.t. 1	1.67	13.82	3.09	6.30
	r^2	0.986	0.743	0.847	0.947
Assets	λ	0.9915	0.7310	0.9300	0.8969
	Standard error	0.0046	0.021	0.021	0.0188
	t-statistic w.r.t. 1	1.85	12.81	3.33	5.49
	r^2	0.996	0.752	0.869	0.844
Employment	λ	0.9741	0.6390	0.9090	0.8716
	Standard error	0.0128	0.024	0.026	0.0331
	t-statistic w.r.t. 1	4.13	15.04	3.50	3.88
	r^2	0.954	0.656	0.783	0.692
Equity	λ	0.9877	0.7590	0.8490	0.8211
	Standard error	0.0101	0.022	0.025	0.0197
	t-statistic w.r.t. 1	1.21	10.95	6.04	9.09
	r^2	0.940	0.752	0.820	0.850

It is possible that a bias is introduced by the method by which the sample was chosen, namely picking the 500 largest firms at the end of the growth period. The smaller of the 500 firms that are included may be in the top 500 because they have been growing at a fast rate. To allow for this possible bias, we examined the ten-year period again but this time chose the firms in accordance with the *Fortune* list of 1963. The results obtained are given in Table 4.3. It is apparent that the values of λ obtained are increased: the value of λ for sales rises from 0.71 to 0.93, that for assets from 0.73 to 0.93, that for employment from 0.64 to 0.91 and that for equity from 0.76 to 0.85. Undoubtedly some sort of bias is introduced by choosing firms on the basis of their size at the end of the sample period. In the short-run – one or two years – this bias would not be important as there would not be sufficient change in the firms included or excluded, but as the time period over which growth is considered becomes longer the difficulty becomes more acute. However, the *t*-statistics with respect to 1 are all still significant – all are greater than 3 – and the results still strongly suggest that small firms grow faster than large firms.

This finding, that small firms grow faster than large firms, is the reverse of what is widely believed – although earlier studies have produced conflicting results. However, it must be stressed that what is meant by 'small' and 'large' here is relative. The firms classified as 'small' may be among the largest in their particular industry so we must be careful in specifying the implications of our results for the behaviour of concentration over time. To see whether concentration is or is not increasing over time in individual industries would involve an industry by industry study that we do not undertake here. What our results do indicate is that for the 500 largest industrial firms the rates of growth of the smaller of these is greater than that of the larger of the firms and this holds irrespective of the measure of firm size used.

5 SIZE AND GROWTH OF FIRMS: EMPIRICAL EVIDENCE FOR THE UNITED KINGDOM

The last column of Table 4.3 reports results for the United Kingdom. Here growth is considered over the years 1971–2 to 1972–3. These results are for the 500 largest firms as in 1972–3.

The results for the United Kingdom are much stronger than the one-year results for the United States. All the λ coefficients are less than one and all are highly significant.

Early studies of U.K. firms by Hart and Prais (1956) and Hart (1962) found values of λ that were less than one but not significantly so; accordingly they concluded that the rate of growth of firms did not vary significantly for firms of different size (i.e. λ = 1). More recent studies by Hart (1965 and 1968), Samuels (1965) and Singh and Whittington (1968) have found that larger firms grow faster (i.e. $\lambda > 1$). An explanation of this, advanced by Samuels (1965), is that since the early fifties there has been a change from proportional growth to large firms growing at a significantly faster rate than small firms and he considers reasons why this might be the case. Finally, we have our results which indicate that small firms grow faster than large firms (i.e. $\lambda > 1$).

We can use our results in section 4.3 to provide a much easier way to reconcile the early studies that found $\lambda = 1$ with later studies that found $\lambda > 1$, obviating the need to suppose – as Samuels did – a structural change. The early studies of Hart and Prais (1956) and Hart (1962) used equity (market value) as their measure of size; the other studies used assets. Denote firm size measures by assets and equity by X_a and X_q respectively so the natural logarithms of the measures are x_a and x_q respectively. We found the following relationship between the two measures

$$x_a = 3.2 + 0.26x_q^{1.7} \qquad (4.20)$$

Then making use of (4.15) we have, where x_a corresponds to x_1 and x_q corresponds to x_2,

$$\frac{\lambda_a}{\lambda_q} = \frac{x_q^{0.7}(t+1)}{x_q^{0.7}(t)} > 1 \qquad (4.21)$$

and so

$$\lambda_a > \lambda_q \qquad (4.22)$$

We may make a crude estimate of λ_a/λ_q, by assuming that from period (t) to period ($t + 1$) market value doubles. The time period used in the various studies differs and hence, the extent of growth as well, but to assume that firm size doubles (on one measure) seems reasonable in light of the studies we are considering here. We make our calculations using the mean value of x_q for our sample and find $\lambda_a/\lambda_q = 1.07$. As an alternative estimate of λ_a/λ_q we may simply take the ratio of estimates from Table 4.3, which gives 1.06. These estimates are consistent with estimates of λ_q slightly below 1 and of λ_a in the range of 1.03 to 1.07 found in the studies cited above. Our results thus provide an explanation of differences in λs found by different researchers without any need to introduce changes in λ over time. That is, the differences in the estimates in earlier studies may be explained purely in terms of differences in the measures of firm size used.

These differences are no help to us, however, in explaining our own results for while the estimated values of λ vary from measure to measure they are all significantly less than unity. Two possible explanations come to mind. First, our firms are large firms, the largest 500 industrial firms. Both Hart and Samuels make use of a sample of firms including firms much smaller than these, and the rates of growth of these firms may be slower than of the firms in the top 500. Secondly, compared with earlier time periods, there may have been a reduction in λ and the rate of growth of firms now decreases with firm size whereas previously it did not.

6 CONCLUSIONS

The conclusions of this chapter are fairly clear-cut. First, that one cannot rely upon a single measure of firm size to assess whether or not there are differences in the growth rates of firms of different size – the interrelationships between different measures are such that incorrect interpretations may arise from the use of a single measure when λ is close to unity, and this seems to have happened in earlier studies. Secondly, there is evidence for both the United States and the United Kingdom that among the group of 500 largest firms in each country the smaller firms in the group are growing faster than the larger ones.

5 Alternative Measures of Concentration: Theory and Evidence

I INTRODUCTION

Various ratios measuring the extent to which control of a market is concentrated have been proposed and used in empirical analysis. Such measures also have considerable practicable importance – for instance in the United States concentration indices play a key role in the implementation of anti-trust laws. Alternative concentration measures differ in their availability and ease of computation and, as choice of the most appropriate concentration measure is an unsettled question, researchers commonly opt for the simplest and most readily available measure – the share of shipments accounted for by the four largest companies in an industry. Support for this position has been provided by evidence that different concentration indices are closely correlated – see Bailey and Boyle (1971). However, arbitrary choice of alternative concentration measures is subject to exactly the same criticism as arbitrary use of firm-size measures. In subsequent sections of this chapter, we shall demonstrate that alternative measures of firm size are readily interchangeable only if they are proportional to each other and we shall show that this condition is not fulfilled for the United States.

2 CONDITIONS UNDER WHICH EMPIRICAL RESULTS WILL BE INDEPENDENT OF THE MEASURE OF CONCENTRATION USED

The most common empirical application of concentration measures is where it is desired to estimate the magnitude of response of some variable to concentration and in particular when it is of interest to ascertain whether the variable varies more than proportionately,

proportionately or less than proportionately with concentration. The most numerous studies of this type are those relating profits to concentration – Bain (1951), Collins and Preston (1966), Fuchs (1961), Kamerschen (1968), Horvath (1970), Levinson (1960), Mann (1966), Miller (1967, 1969, 1971), Ornstein (1972), Stigler (1963) and Weiss (1963, 1971). Other studies relate to concentration variables such as margins, capital barriers, labour factors and wage and price variables – Comanor and Wilson (1967), Scherer (1973), Sherman and Tollison (1971) and Weiss (1961).

The formal analysis of the conditions under which alternative concentration indices may be interchanged, i.e. conclusions are independent of the concentration measure used, is identical with that for the conditions under which it is legitimate to interchange measures of firm size. Some of the analysis that we shall do is easier with a model expressed in actual values and some of the analysis is easier with a logarithmic model so we shall present both.

Consider two alternative measures of concentration

$$C_1 = a + bC_2 \tag{5.1}$$

where b is positive. If we fit

$$Y = g + hC_1 \tag{5.2}$$

where h is positive then, depending on whether g is negative, zero or positive we conclude that Y increases more than proportionately, proportionately or less than proportionately to C_1. Now substituting for C_1 from (5.1) in (5.2) gives

$$Y = (g + ah) + bhC_2 \tag{5.3}$$

Y increases more than proportionately, proportionately or less than proportionately to C_2 depending on whether $g + ah$ is negative, zero or positive. Only if a is zero does $g = g + ah$ (for non-zero h) so that there is no ambiguity about the elasticity between Y and concentration.

Consider now the same effect with a logarithmic model where

$$C_1 = AC_2^\beta \tag{5.4}$$

and A and β are positive. Taking natural logarithms, denoted by lower-case letters, and writing $\alpha = \ln A$ we have

$$c_1 = \alpha + \beta c_2 \tag{5.5}$$

If we fit

$$y = \gamma + \delta c_1 \qquad (5.6)$$

which implies

$$Y = \Gamma c_1^{\delta} \qquad (5.7)$$

then substituting for c_1 from (5.5) gives

$$y = \gamma + \alpha\delta + \beta\delta c_2 \qquad (5.8)$$

and the two concentration indices will yield the same elasticity for Y with respect to concentration only if, for non-zero δ, $\beta = 1$, i.e. they are proportional to each other.

3 DISCRETE AND CONTINUOUS CONCENTRATION MEASURES

Our analysis deals with eight concentration measures taken from two general classes of concentration ratios – discrete and cumulative measures.*

The most common type of discrete concentration measure shows the proportion of total industry value of shipments accounted for by the n largest firms. Thus any such measure, CR_n, is given by

$$CR_n = \sum_{i=1}^{n} X_i \Big/ \sum_{i=1}^{m} X_m \qquad (5.9)$$

where X_i denotes shipments by firm i, firms 1 to n are the n largest firms and the industry consists of m firms. A merit of these measures is that they are easy to compute and require only details of shipments for the industry as a whole and for the n firms. The strongest argument against the discrete measures is that it is difficult to see how satisfactory judgement on changes in monopolistic tendencies in an industry can be made without knowledge of changes in the number of firms engaged in that industry.

We shall consider four discrete concentration measures – they measure the share of value of shipments accounted for by the 4, 8, 20 and 50 largest manufacturing companies in an industry; we denote these measures by CR_4, CR_8, CR_{20}, CR_{50} respectively.

Cumulative measures take into account not merely the number of firms in an industry but also the entire size distribution of firms. The

* For discussions of measures of concentration see, *inter alia*, Rosenbluth (1955), Stigler (1955), Hall and Tideman (1967), Horvath (1970), Adelman (1969), Eveley and Little (1960) and Bailey and Boyle (1971).

major disadvantage of cumulative concentration measures is that they are cumbersome to construct; this in large part accounts for the heavy reliance that has been placed on discrete measures. The cumulative measures that we consider here are based on the Herfindahl index defined as

$$HF_n = \sum_{i=1}^{n} z_i^2 \qquad (5.10)$$

where n is the number of firms over which the index is calculated ($n \leq m$, the number of firms in the industry) and z_i is the decimal fraction of industry shipments belonging to firm i, that is

$$z_i = X_i \Big/ \sum_{=1}^{m} X_i \qquad (5.11)$$

A variety of possible firm-size distributions have been suggested in measuring concentration. We shall limit our discussion to the assumption introduced by Hall and Tideman (1967) which is that each firm has a size equal to the mean of its size class. We shall denote such an Herfindahl index by HFM_n. Assumptions about firm-size distributions are necessary, for usually the available data are in grouped form. A basic data source for the study of concentration in the United States is *Concentration Ratios in Manufacturing Industry* (1970). In that publication, firms are grouped by size classes, the classes being 1 to 4, 5 to 8, 9 to 20, 21 to 50, 51 to m, and in our analysis, we shall consider these size classes although our theoretical analysis could be set up with any structure of size classes.

It is convenient to denote the mean decimal proportion of total shipments by firms in the five size classes by $\bar{z}_4$, $\bar{z}_8$, $\bar{z}_{20}$, $\bar{z}_{50}$ and $\bar{z}_m$ respectively. Then the proportion of shipments accounted for by each size class is given by $4\bar{z}_4$, $4\bar{z}_8$, $12\bar{z}_{20}$, $30\bar{z}_{50}$ and $(m - 50)\bar{z}_m$ respectively. The four discrete concentration indices that we consider here are given by

$$CR_4 = 4\bar{z}_4 \qquad (5.12)$$

$$CR_8 = 4\bar{z}_4 + 4\bar{z}_8 \qquad (5.13)$$

$$CR_{20} = 4\bar{z}_4 + 4\bar{z}_8 + 12\bar{z}_{20} \qquad (5.14)$$

$$CR_{50} = 4\bar{z}_4 + 4\bar{z}_8 + 12\bar{z}_{20} + 30\bar{z}_{50} \qquad (5.15)$$

By substituting for $4\bar{z}_4$ from (5.13) into (5.12), we obtain

$$CR_4 = CR_8 - 4\bar{z}_8 \qquad (5.16)$$

Similarly from (5.14) and (5.12), we get

$$CR_4 = CR_{20} - 4\bar{z}_8 - 12\bar{z}_{20} \qquad (5.17)$$

Clearly we can express any CR_n in terms of similar indices with different values of n and obtain the matrix in Table 5.1. Each relation in this table is similar to equation (5.1) above, with the value of a being negative. Thus we know that the four concentration indices are not proportional to each other, for proportionality requires $a = 0$; hence the conditions for interchangeability are not met and conclusions of empirical studies will not be independent of the measure of concentration used. In addition we know the qualitative relationship between the measures and hence what the effect of the use of alternative concentration measures in relationships like (5.3) will be. As a is negative the elasticity of any index CR_n with another index CR_{n+k}, where k is positive, is greater than one. In (5.3), the larger k is in the CR_{n+k} measure used as C_2, the larger, in absolute terms, is the negative coefficient a and hence the larger will be the elasticity of Y with respect to CR_{n+k} relative to the elasticity of Y with respect to CR_n.

TABLE 5.1

Relationship between discrete
concentration measures

$CR_4 = CR_8 - 4\bar{z}_8 = CR_{20} - 4\bar{z}_8 - 12\bar{z}_{20} = CR_{50} - 4\bar{z}_8 - 4\bar{z}_{20} - 30\bar{z}_{50}$
$CR_8 = \qquad\qquad = CR_{20} - 12\bar{z}_{20} \qquad = CR_{50} - 12\bar{z}_{20} - 30\bar{z}_{50}$
$CR_{20} = \qquad\qquad\qquad\qquad\qquad\qquad = CR_{50} - 30\bar{z}_{50}$

We now turn to a comparison of the Herfindahl indices where it is assumed that each firm has a size equal to the mean of its size class. Then we have

$$HFM_4 = 4\bar{z}_4^2 \qquad (5.18)$$

$$HFM_8 = 4\bar{z}_4^2 + 4\bar{z}_8^2 \qquad (5.19)$$

$$HFM_{20} = 4\bar{z}_4^2 + 4\bar{z}_8^2 + 12\bar{z}_{20}^2 \qquad (5.20)$$

$$HFM_{50} = 4\bar{z}_4^2 + 4\bar{z}_8^2 + 12\bar{z}_{20}^2 + 30\bar{z}_{50}^2 \qquad (5.21)$$

$$HFM_m = 4\bar{z}_4^2 + 4\bar{z}_8^2 + 12\bar{z}_{20}^2 + 30\bar{z}_{50}^2 + (m - 50)\bar{z}_m^2 \qquad (5.22)$$

Clearly this gives us the same general type of pattern as between the discrete indices, and similar conclusions follow.*

We may make a theoretical comparison between any CR index and any HFM index and demonstrate that they are not proportional. Especially interesting is a comparison of the CR_4 index with the HFM_4 index because we find a fixed relation between them. Manipulating (5.18), we have

$$\bar{z}_4 = 0.5HFM^{0.5}_4 \qquad (5.23)$$

Substituting for $\bar{z}_4$ from (5.23) into (5.12) gives

$$CR_4 = 2HFM^{0.5}_4 \qquad (5.24)$$

This is our logarithmic form, equation (5.4), with β, the elasticity between CR_4 and HFM_4, equal to $\frac{1}{2}$. The elasticity between other CR and HFM measures will depend on the values of $\bar{z}_8$, $\bar{z}_{20}$, $\bar{z}_{50}$ and $\bar{z}_{m-50}$ but they will not be proportional because all the HFM indices involve terms in $\bar{z}_n^2$. For instance we have

$$\begin{aligned} CR_8 &= 4\bar{z}_4 + 4\bar{z}_8 \\ &= CR_4 + 4\bar{z}_8 \\ &= 2HFM^{0.5}_4 + 4\bar{z}_8 \end{aligned} \qquad (5.25)$$

4 EMPIRICAL EVIDENCE

The theoretical analysis of the previous section has demonstrated that the conditions necessary for interchangeability of concentration measures will not be fulfilled. Except for the comparison of CR_4 with HFM_4, however, we do not know the magnitude of these effects. Accordingly we now present some empirical evidence for the United States; data limitations preclude a similar analysis for the United Kingdom.

Our data source is *Concentration Ratios in Manufacturing Industry*

* Two alternative firm-size distributions have been proposed by Bailey and Boyle (1971, p. 704). In the first the four largest firms are distributed linearly so that the fourth firm has the same size as the mean of the next smallest size class; all firms in the smaller size classes are distributed in such a way that they are assumed to be equal to the mean of their size class. In the second proposed distribution the largest firm is allowed to be as large as possible (but not over 50 per cent of the industry total) and the second, third and fourth firm sizes are distributed equally (but not so that they are smaller than the next size class) and the other firms are distributed as the means of their size classes. For these distributions the algebra is much more complicated but it is possible to show that the resulting indices are not in general proportional to each other or to other indices,

(1970, part 1, Table 4). Measures are derived for Census 4-digit industries and the sample size is 390 throughout.

As in Chapter 3 we fit orthogonal regressions to logarithmic data. Table 5.2 presents our results. In each cell in that table the first line gives the orthogonal regression coefficient between the measure listed on the left and the measure listed above, the second line gives the standard error of the regression coefficient and the final line gives the t-statistic calculated with respect to unity. All the t-statistics with respect to 1 are very high, the smallest being 13.99. The results fall into three groups. First, the coefficients between the various CR measures; here the coefficients vary from 1.13 to 2.00. Secondly, the

TABLE 5.2

Orthogonal regression coefficients:
alternative measures of concentration

	CR_8	CR_{20}	CR_{50}	HFM_4	HFM_8	HFM_{20}	HFM_{50}
CR_4	1.1301	1.4350	2.0001	0.5003	0.5278	0.5618	0.5877
	0.0093	0.0237	0.0552	0.0060	0.0021	0.0032	0.0038
	13.99	18.35	18.12	83.38	224.85	136.94	108.50
CR_8		1.2554	1.7150	0.4394	0.4671	0.4774	0.5210
		0.0118	0.0376	0.0037	0.0024	0.0023	0.0029
		21.64	19.02	151.51	222.04	227.22	165.17
CR_{20}			1.3331	0.3410	0.3653	0.3918	0.4101
			0.0206	0.0056	0.0049	0.0046	0.0049
			16.17	117.68	129.53	132.29	120.39
CR_{50}				0.2405	0.2592	0.2797	0.2928
				0.0372	0.0065	0.0066	0.0069
				20.42	113.97	109.14	102.49
HFM_4					1.0569	1.1274	1.1804
					0.0039	0.0062	0.0072
					14.59	20.55	25.06
HFM_8						1.0661	1.1160
						0.0025	0.0037
						26.44	31.35
HFM_{20}							1.0466
							0.0016
							29.13

Note: In each cell the first row is the orthogonal regression coefficient indicating the elasticity of the measure listed on the left to the measure listed above; the second row is the standard error; the third row is the t-value calculated with respect to an elasticity of unity.

coefficients between the *HFM* measures; the range here is smaller and the various Herfindahl measures that we have calculated seem good substitutes for each other. Finally, we have the comparison of the *CR* measures with the *HFM* measures. Here the differences are very marked; the closest coefficient to 1 is that between CR_4 and HFM_{50} and that is as low as 0.59, and the smallest coefficient is 0.24, that between CR_{50} and HFM_4. Taking the reciprocals of these, which is equivalent to calculating the elasticity between the *HFM* measures and the *CR* measures, we have a range of 1.70 to 4.16.

The results of our empirical analysis are fairly clear-cut. The Herfindahl indices that we have calculated are the best substitutes for each other although a difference of nearly 20 per cent results from interchanging HFM_4 and HFM_{50}. Marked differences in conclusions would be reached depending on which concentration measure was used in a study. And quite extreme differences in conclusions would result depending on whether a discrete measure of concentration (a *CR* measure) was used or a Herfindahl measure.

5 IMPLICATIONS OF THE RESULTS

We have demonstrated that conclusions from empirical studies using concentration indices will be sensitive to the measure of concentration used. A couple of examples may be helpful.

A number of studies in which profitability was found to increase with the degree of concentration were cited earlier in this chapter. Some of these studies have used a particular measure of concentration because it was most conveniently available, most commonly CR_4, when a more appropriate measure to use on theoretical grounds would be a more complex measure such as the Herfindahl measure. The elasticity of CR_4 with respect to all the *HFM* measures in Table 5.2 is less than 1, in the range 0.50 to 0.59, so it follows that if a Herfindahl measure were used instead of CR_4, profitability would increase more slowly with concentration than was estimated.

An explicit example of the implications of our results is provided in the study by Miller (1967) of profit rates and concentration ratios. Miller obtains a positive relationship between profit rates and the concentration ratios CR_4 and CR_8 where profit rates increase less than proportionally with concentration. Using two measures of profit rates, Miller obtains with each measure a more than proportional response of profit rates to concentration and a larger response when concentration is measured by CR_8 than when concentration is measures by CR_4. The results in Table 5.2 explain the Miller results simply from the relationship between CR_4 and CR_8; CR_4 increases less than proportionately with CR_8.

A final example of the implication of our results can be seen in the Collins and Preston study (1966) of profitability and concentration. They conclude that an increase of 10 percentage points in concentration leads to an increase of almost 1 percentage point in price–cost margins. From Table 5.1, this result would not hold had Collins and Preston used a measure other than CR_4; their relationship would have shown less of an increase in price–cost margins in response to an increase in concentration – from 12 to 20 per cent if other concentration-ratio measures were used and from 5 to 6 per cent had one of the Herfindahl measures been used.

So far we have discussed the effects of interchanging measures when those measures are used as independent variables. In some cases it is desired to use a concentration measure as the dependent variable; in particular, many studies have attempted to explain the variation of concentration ratios with the variation in advertising intensities – Marcus (1971), Comanor and Wilson (1967), Kaldor (1950) and Guth (1971). These studies have shown that advertising affects the distribution of firm sizes in an industry. The percentage increase in concentration that comes with a percentage increase in advertising is important; it indicates the speed of the effect on the distribution of firms and hence has implications for the law of proportionate effect. For example, let us fit

$$\ln CR_8 = 10.0 + 8.1 \ln A_D$$

where A_D is the measure of advertising intensity and the coefficients 10.0 and 8.1 are drawn from Marcus (1971). Now, from Table 5.2, use of a measure other than CR_8 could alter the elasticity anywhere between 2.0 and 14.2 (rather than 8.1), thus drastically changing the response of concentration to changes in advertising.

6 CONCLUSIONS

For empirical results to be independent of the choice of measure of concentration a quite stringent condition must hold. It is not sufficient that the measures are highly correlated. The necessary and sufficient condition for measures to be interchangeable is that they be proportional. It follows simply from the definitions of the measures that measures cannot be proportional to each other and so this condition cannot be fulfilled. Our examination of eight concentration measures for 390 4-digit industries for the United States has demonstrated that the divergence from proportionality is marked. Accordingly, choice of concentration measure will have considerable impact on the conclusions of empirical studies.

6 Profitability, Size and Concentration

I INTRODUCTION

In this chapter, we investigate the influence of firm size and industrial concentration on firm profitability.

In a perfectly competitive world, profit rates tend to equality. As imperfect markets are taken into account the size of a firm must be considered as a factor in producing profits. Baumol (1967) suggested that the larger firm may be in a position to earn a higher rate of return on its investment than the smaller firm because it has all the options of a smaller firm open to it and in addition can undertake projects that are of such large scale that they are denied to smaller firms. A similar argument had earlier been put forward by Steindl (1945). A counter-argument is that size breeds inefficiency and that, accordingly, large firms cannot undertake the options open to a small firm as efficiently as the small firm and hence profitability may decline with size of firms. Also Benishay (1961) has argued that the stock market will tend to favour large firms so that there will be a negative relationship between profitability and equity.

Thus we find that some theoretical arguments suggest that profitability should increase with firm size; others suggest a negative relationship.

Profitability may be expected to be directly related to the monopoly power of a firm. The proposition often stated is that the level of concentration affects the interdependence among firms and therefore the closeness of their market performance to the theoretical monopoly solution. A common way of measuring monopoly power is by the use of indices of concentration and we shall follow this procedure. The hypothesis generally investigated is that the firms in more highly concentrated industries are in a position to create higher profit rates than firms in less concentrated industries.

We shall not run separate regressions for individual industries or include dummy variables to represent industries for two reasons. First, the major reason why we should expect inter-industry differences in profitability is that there are differences in the degree of monopoly power in different industries and we are including concentration indices to take account of this. Secondly, there is the evidence of Gort and Singamsetti (1974) who use a data set for the United States that is adjusted to allow for the fact that individual corporations frequently operate in more than one industry. Using an analysis of variance approach they find that

> the industry of a firm is not a dominant variable in determining profit rate levels. . . . Even more striking is the fact that the proportion of the total variance explained by industry means does not rise as the level of industry detail increases. . . . This reinforces the conclusion that the role of industry and market characteristics in determining the level of profit rates is relatively weak, on the average, as compared to the role of variables that pertain to individual firms.*

2 SURVEY OF PREVIOUS STUDIES

Before undertaking our own analysis we shall briefly report the results of previous studies.

In their study for the United Kingdom, Samuels and Smyth (1968) used data for 186 companies drawn from manufacturing, distribution and mining and covering the period 1954–63. The firms were ranked into ten size classes by their 1954 net assets. The firms ranged in size from the very large (over £65 million in assets) to small firms (less than £0.25 million in assets). Analysis of variance indicated that size was a significant factor in the determination of mean profitability (measured as the ratio of profits after depreciation but before taxation to net assets) over the ten-year period. This finding was further supported when similar analyses of variance were undertaken for each individual year. Profitability of companies tended to increase up to £1 million or £2 million of net assets and then declined.† For the range of large companies that we are considering in this book Samuels and Smyth found profitability to decline with firm size.

A negative relationship between profitability and size was also

---

* Gort and Singamsetti (1974, p. 11).
† For some implications of the results see Jay (1972, pp. 14ff.).

found for the United Kingdom by Singh and Whittington (1968) although their study was limited to four industries and by Radice (1972) in his analysis of 68 firms but in his study in no case was the coefficient of size significant at the 5 per cent level.

We now turn to the U.S. studies. We shall consider only those studies that use data for individual firms, as we do, not those based on aggregative Internal Revenue Service data – studies using Internal Revenue Service data include Crum (1939), Marcus (1969), Stekler (1963, 1964) and Stigler (1963).

In an early study of 56 companies, Benishay (1961) found a strong negative relationship between profitability and size measured by equity. Benishay's analysis was for 56 companies in the four years, 1954, 1955, 1956 and 1957; his measure of profitability was the ratio of post-tax profits to equity.

Hall and Weiss (1967), using assets as the size measure and the ratio of profits to invested capital as the profit-rate measure, found a significant and positive relationship between profit rates and firm size. Their sample consisted of firms that were listed in *Fortune*'s top 400 firms at least once during the seven-year period 1956–62. This means that firms were considered as separate observations anywhere from one to seven times. Hall and Weiss do not consider the difficulties introduced into their analysis by this combination of time-series and cross-section data. A fair amount of literature has been developed around the efficient combination of cross-section and time-series data beginning with Hoch's analysis of covariance approach (1962) and more recently with Maddala (1971). While we cannot consider *a priori* the biases in their results we do avoid a similar problem by considering just the cross-section sample and not combining a number of years.

One other difficulty of the Hall and Weiss sample is that in their time-series and cross-section sample, no consideration is given to the entry and exit of firms into and out of the top 400 firms. These factors could imply relative overstatement of the profit rate to firm-size relationship since over time the average profit rate of all firms follows the business cycle which was generally up during 1956–62, and over the period the average firm size of the top 400 firms was also increasing. For example, from 1955 (when *Fortune* began compiling the list) to 1973 the sales cut-off point for inclusion in the top 500 has risen 310 per cent or an average annual increase of 8.2 per cent.

Kamerschen (1968) related profit rates to firm size and other variables for 47 of the largest 200 non-financial corporations for the period 1959–64, using total assets and sales as firm-size measures and the ratio of profits to invested capital as the profit-rate measure. He found significant positive relationships between firm size and profit rates but his analysis is subject to a similar criticism as the Hall and Weiss study.

Most of the studies relating profitability to concentration have used industry data. We shall not consider these here, limiting our discussion to those studies that have used data at the firm level.*

For the period 1936–40, Bain (1951) found average profit rates to be higher for firms classified into a high-concentration group than for those classified into a low-concentration group.

Miller (1967) found a positive relationship between profitability and concentration, measuring concentration by CR_4 and CR_8.

Hall and Weiss (1967), using a modification of CR_4, found the influence of concentration to be significant but small.

Kamerschen (1968) found no significant relationship between profitability and concentration when other variables were included. His measure of concentration was CR_8.

Arnould and Fletcher (1972), using as their measure of concentration CR_4, found a weak positive relationship between concentration and profitability in food processing.

Finally, Gort and Singamsetti (1974) classified firms into high and low-concentration industries. They used CR_8 and tried various ways of classification and found that the differences in profit rates between firms in more and less concentrated industries were small for all measures of concentration and profit rates.

3 THE DATA

The set of firms analysed is the same as in Chapter 3. We consider the 500 largest industrial corporations in the United Kingdom and the United States, extending our analysis to the 100 largest U.K. firms for one year, 1971–2.

The measures of firm size used are those described in Chapter 3. In view of our findings in that chapter it is clearly wise to repeat the analysis using each measure of firm size.

We make use of the measures of profits given in *The Times 1000*

* For a survey of some of the evidence using industry data see Yamey (1972).

and in *Fortune 500*. For the United Kingdom, profits are defined as net profit before interest and tax; the U.S. definition is profits after taxes and after extraordinary credits or charges when they are shown on the income statement.

If the income tax treatment of different companies is similar it seems inconsequential whether profits are measured before or after tax. This is the case for the United Kingdom. However, there are inter-industry differences in tax treatment for the United States, for instance, the oil-depletion allowance for firms in the oil industry, so post-tax profits are appropriate for the United States.

Differences in the treatment of interest payments in arriving at profitability mean that the measure of the rate of return is to some extent sensitive to the method of financing. Large companies on average have a higher capital gearing* than smaller companies and differences in gearing may explain some differences in the rate of return of companies of different size, but the effect is not likely to be of major importance – see Samuels and Smyth (1968, p. 128).

We wish to compare the rate of return to size of firm and concentration. We may measure profitability, the rate of return, by taking the ratio of profits to either equity or to assets. In order to see if the behaviour of profitability is independent of the measure of profitability used we shall undertake our analysis using both measures.

The rate of return on equity may be preferred to the rate of return on assets as the measure of profitability as it is what profit maximisers might be expected to maximise and invested capital is what is at risk in a firm – see Friedman and Friedman (1972). It should be noted that assets are not an entirely satisfactory base for profit comparisons, as assets may not be valued properly. The basis for some assets are historical cost and for others replacement value, and some firms are more capital-intensive than others. Over a period of sustained inflation firms with relatively old assets will report smaller assets than firms with recently acquired assets. Firms undertake asset revisions but the timing of such revisions is irregular.

For the United Kingdom, we do not have equity for unquoted companies so our sample size is smaller for the regressions measuring the rate of return on equity than for the regressions measuring rate of return on assets. When equity is used as the measure of firm size in the regressions in which profitability is measured by the ratio of profits to assets the number of observations are also reduced.

* In the United States, for 'gearing' read 'leverage'.

Tables 3.1 and 3.2 indicate the sample sizes for the regressions involving profitability and size and excluding concentration.

In view of the results in Chapter 5, we wish to repeat our analysis using different measures of concentration. This is possible for the United States but not for the United Kingdom.

For the United States our data source for the measures of concentration are the same as in Chapter 5. The 4-, 8-, 20- and 50-firm concentration measures are reported by 4-digit SIC code for 390 industries and we constructed 4-, 8-, 20- and 50-firm Herfindahl indices for each industry. Using SIC codes, we assigned the appropriate concentration indices to each firm. As some firms were not classified by SIC code and as concentration indices were not reported for some SIC codes the sample size was reduced when a measure of concentration was included as a variable. For instance, the sample size for 1972 was reduced to 427.

Our problems were greatly increased for the United Kingdom as concentration indices are not readily available. We adopted the 4-firm indices constructed by Sawyer (1971) and classified each firm into an industry and assigned the appropriate index to each firm where possible. However, as the number of industries for which indices were constructed was small, 125, and the classification of firms into industries was often difficult, the sample size was quite reduced when a concentration measure was included in a regression. For instance, concentration indices were assigned to only 317 firms in 1972–3.

4 PROFITABILITY, CONCENTRATION AND SIZE: EMPIRICAL EVIDENCE FOR THE UNITED KINGDOM

We first fit the following models

$$P/X_a = a_0 + a_1 x_i + a_2(cr_4) \qquad (6.1)$$

and

$$P/X_q = b_0 + b_1 x_i + b_2(cr_4) \qquad (6.2)$$

where P denotes profits, X_a and X_q the value of assets and equity respectively, x_i the natural logarithm of the measure of firm size used (where i denotes sales, assets, employment or equity) and cr_4 the natural logarithm of the 4-firm concentration measure, CR_4.

Table 6.1 gives the results for equation (6.1) for 1972–3; t-values of the regression coefficients are given under the coefficients. It is apparent that the concentration measure is not significant. Regressions for 1970–71 and 1971–2 also give coefficients for cr_4 that are not significant. Similarly, when equation (6.2) is fitted for the three years with different size measures, the coefficients for cr_4 are not significant. We thus conclude that, for large U.K. industrial companies, profitability does not depend on concentration and we shall therefore devote the rest of this section to a consideration of results with the concentration variable excluded. This permits us to consider a larger sample of firms.

TABLE 6.1

Profitability, size and concentration:
United Kingdom, 1972–3, profitability
measured by profits/assets

Size Measure	ln Size	lnCR_4	R^2
Sales	− 0.0050	0.0052	0.006
	− 0.89	0.84	
Assets	− 0.0194	0.0155	0.062
	− 4.56	0.26	
Employment	− 0.0096	0.0048	0.018
	− 2.17	0.80	
Equity	0.0063	0.0052	0.025
	3.51	0.80	

Note: In each cell the first row gives the regression coefficient and the second row the t-statistic.

Table 6.2 gives the results for the three years 1970–71, 1971–2 and 1972–3 with the profits/assets ratio as the dependent variable. In each cell the first row gives the coefficient of the natural logarithm of the firm-size measure, the second row the t-statistic and the third row the R^2. We also estimated non-linear regressions by adding the square of the logarithm of firm size but in no case was this additional term significant at the 5 per cent level. The evidence in Table 6.2 supports a positive relationship between profitability and equity, a negative one between profitability and assets and between profitability and employment, and, more weakly, a negative one between profitability and sales. The results are quite consistent for the different years. The results for the largest 1000 firms are similar to those for the largest 500 firms except that the relationship between profitability and employment is not significant with the largest 1000 firms while it is with the largest 500.

TABLE 6.2

Profitability and size: United Kingdom,
profitability measured by
profits/assets

Size measure	500 largest industrial companies			1000 largest industrial companies
	1970–1	1971–2	1972–3	1971–2
ln Sales	− 0.0104 − 2.26 0.013	− 0.0084 − 1.58 0.005	− 0.0042 − 0.85 0.001	− 0.0059 − 1.92 0.004
ln Assets	− 0.0186 − 5.58 0.060	− 0.0153 − 3.22 0.051	− 0.0179 − 5.02 0.048	− 0.0164 − 3.42 0.035
ln Employment	− 0.0116 − 2.92 0.029	− 0.0107 − 4.07 0.032	− 0.0065 − 2.71 0.015	− 0.0006 − 0.47 0.003
ln Equity	0.0044 2.41 0.013	0.0030 1.57 0.005	0.0056 3.42 0.023	0.0069 4.87 0.027

Note: In each cell the first row gives the coefficient of the natural logarithm of the size measure; the second row gives the *t*-statistic; the third row gives the R^2.

In Table 6.3, we present the results of the regressions with the ratio of profits to equity as the dependent variable. Here all the coefficients are negative and all are significant at the 5 per cent level except the sales and assets coefficients for 1972–3.

Note the striking difference in the results obtained with size measured by equity for the two measures of profitability – profitability measured by profits/assets is positively related to equity while profitability measured by profits/equity is negatively related to equity, and both sets of relationships are highly significant.

5 PROFITABILITY, CONCENTRATION AND SIZE: EMPIRICAL EVIDENCE FOR THE UNITED STATES

We fit the following models

$$P/X_a = a_0 + a_1 x_i + a_2 c_j \tag{6.3}$$

and

$$P/X_q = b_0 + b_1 x_i + b_2 c_j \qquad (6.4)$$

where c_j denotes the natural logarithm of the measure of concentration used (CR_4, CR_8, CR_{20}, CR_{50}, HFM_4, HFM_8, HFM_{20} or HFM_{50}).

TABLE 6.3

Profitability and size: United Kingdom,
profitability measured by profits/equity

Size measure	500 largest industrial companies			1000 largest industrial companies
	1970–71	1971–2	1972–3	1971–2
ln Sales	− 1.6698	− 1.5687	− 0.1678	− 1.6132
	− 2.23	− 2.21	− 0.34	− 2.41
	0.013	0.013	0.002	0.021
ln Assets	− 1.6827	− 1.6238	− 0.4674	− 1.6415
	− 2.98	− 3.04	− 1.25	− 3.71
	0.023	0.024	0.004	0.032
ln Employment	− 2.2800	− 2.5748	− 1.0747	− 2.6476
	− 3.88	− 4.77	− 2.74	− 4.98
	0.038	0.057	0.021	0.091
ln Equity	− 4.030	− 3.2361	− 1.8306	− 3.4163
	− 8.67	− 7.30	− 5.49	− 7.61
	0.166	0.125	0.078	0.163

Note: In each cell the first row gives the coefficient of the natural logarithm of the size measure; the second row gives the t-statistic; the third row gives the R^2.

Table 6.4 gives the t-statistics for different concentration measures combined with different size measures for 1972 where profits/equity is the dependent variable. It is apparent that none of the t-values are significant. Similar results are obtained for 1965, 1968 and 1970 and for all four years when profits/assets is used as the dependent variable. In view of the lack of significance of the concentration coefficients, we shall now consider results of regressions that exclude the concentration variables as this will permit us to consider a larger sample of firms.

Table 6.5 gives the results for the four years 1965, 1968, 1970 and 1972 with the profits/assets ratio as the dependent variable. In each cell the first row gives the coefficient of the natural logarithm of the firm-size measure, the second row the t-statistic and the third row the R^2. The relationship between profitability and equity is a positive one in all years and the regression coefficients are significant at the 5 per cent level for all but 1972. None of the regression coefficients for other size measures are significantly different from zero at the 5 per cent level although the coefficients for assets are all negative, and

TABLE 6.4

Profitability, size and concentration; t-statistics
for concentration variables, 1972

Size measure included in regressions	Concentration measure							
	ln CR_4	ln CR_8	ln CR_{20}	ln CR_{50}	ln HFM_4	ln HFM_8	ln HFM_{20}	ln HFM_{50}
ln Sales	−0.67	−0.66	−0.63	−0.60	−0.72	−0.72	−0.70	−0.66
ln Assets	−0.66	−0.64	−0.61	−0.59	−0.70	−0.69	−0.66	−0.64
ln Employment	−0.63	−0.63	−0.64	−0.58	−0.68	−0.69	−0.65	−0.61
ln Equity	−0.85	−0.84	−0.80	−0.76	−0.91	−0.89	−0.87	−0.83

TABLE 6.5

Profitability and size: United States,
profitability measured by
profits/assets

	1965	1968	1970	1972
Sales	−0.0061 −0.53 0.002	−0.0094 −0.40 0.002	−0.0028 −1.39 0.001	0.0013 0.41 0.001
Assets	−0.0021 −1.91 0.011	−0.0018 −1.87 0.008	−0.0021 −1.21 0.003	−0.0026 −1.96 0.008
Employment	−0.0013 −0.69 0.001	−0.0049 −2.00 0.009	−0.0018 −0.99 0.002	−0.0029 −0.74 0.002
Equity	0.0041 2.11 0.011	0.0032 1.99 0.003	0.0038 2.34 0.012	0.0025 1.14 0.003

Note: In each cell the first row gives the coefficient of the natural logarithm of the size measure; the second row gives the t-statistic; the third row gives the R^2.

three of them are fairly close to significance indicating some negative relationship between profits/assets and assets.

Table 6.6 gives the corresponding results when the profits/equity ratio is the dependent variable. The coefficients obtained for equity are all negative and significant at the 5 per cent level for all four years. None of the coefficients for the other size variables are significant at the 5 per cent level in any year.

TABLE 6.6
Profitability and size: United States,
profitability measured by
profits/equity

	1965	1968	1970	1972
Sales	− 0.0071 − 0.93 0.002	0.0029 0.41 0.002	0.0031 0.39 0.001	− 0.0096 − 0.89 0.002
Assets	− 0.0094 − 1.14 0.004	0.0052 0.71 0.002	0.0068 0.10 0.001	− 0.0109 − 1.19 0.003
Employment	− 0.0103 − 1.132 0.003	0.0022 0.76 0.002	0.0014 0.18 0.001	− 0.0147 − 1.04 0.002
Equity	− 0.0481 − 4.10 0.037	− 0.0142 − 3.42 0.024	− 0.0224 − 3.54 0.028	− 0.1789 − 5.82 0.045

Note: In each cell the first row gives the coefficient of the natural logarithm of the size measure; the second row gives the t-statistic; the third row gives the R^2.

We also fitted non-linear regressions by including the square of the logarithm of the size variable. The general tendency was for the co-efficient of the logarithm of size to be positive and for that of the square of the logarithm of size to be negative but for the coefficients not to be significant. However, when profits/equity was the dependent variable and equity the size variable the linear term was negative, and the squared term was positive, both regression coefficients being significant.

6 CONCLUSIONS

Clearly, whether one concludes that profitability increases or decreases with firm size or is independent of firm size depends on how profitability is measured and what measure of firm size is used. These results help to explain the conflicting results of earlier studies. In both countries, profitability measured by profits/equity are negatively and highly significantly related to size measured by equity, whereas profits/assets are positively and usually significantly related to equity. In the United Kingdom both profits/assets and profits/equity are negatively and significantly related to size measured by sales, assets and employment. In the United States when size is measured by sales, assets or employment, there is a tendency for a negative relationship when profits/assets is the profitability measure; there are no significant relationships with these size variables when profits/equity is the profitability measure.

Even in those regressions where the size variables are significant the R^2s are very low, making it clear that size differences account for only a small proportion of inter-firm differences in profitability. In this context it should be noted that the higher R^2s in some earlier studies are misleading. For instance, the Hall and Weiss regressions include dummy variables reflecting years so that most of the variance of profit rates explained in their analysis is due to cyclical movements in the profit rates of firms of all sizes and not to inter-firm profitability differences.

There is no evidence that industry concentration influences profitability in either the United Kingdom or the United States.

7 Variability of Profits and Firm Size

I INTRODUCTION AND DATA

In this chapter, we investigate two questions for the 500 largest U.K. and U.S. industrial firms. First, when firms are grouped into size classes does the variability of profit rates between firms in each size class differ between groups? Secondly, does the variability of profit rates for firms in different size classes differ over time? To examine these questions, we use an analysis of variance approach. For the United States, we also present some evidence based on a comparison of time series for individual firms examining also the hypothesis that profit variability depends on concentration. Finally, for the United States, we see if there is a trade-off between profitability and the variability of profitability.

For the analysis of variance approach, we use sales as a measure of firm size. Because we are merely comparing variances and not estimating specific functional forms or elasticities, the problems raised in Chapters 2 and 3 concerning the measurement of firm size are avoided. As sales is the size measure by which firms are ranked in *The Times 1000* and in *Fortune 500*, classification by sales provides the most simple separation into firm-size classes. In the latter part of the chapter, where regression analysis is used, it is necessary to repeat the regressions using all four measures of firm size, not just sales.

The U.K. data cover the three years 1969–70, 1970–71 and 1971–72; this part of the analysis was completed before 1972–73 data were available. The period 1969–72 was one of rather irregular growth – the rate of capacity utilisation fell and seasonally adjusted constant-price gross domestic product declined from the second half of 1970 to the first half of 1971. The data are from *The Times 1000* and its predecessor, *The Times 500*.

The U.S. data cover the time period 1960 to 1968; this period was chosen because *Fortune 500* data on magnetic tape were available to us for those years. The time period is one which includes all phases of the cycle – in 1960–61 there was a recession (as defined by the National Bureau of Economic Research), 1961–66 was a period of sustained growth in gross national product, in 1967 there was a 'growth recession' and 1968 was a year of recovery from this.

2 INTER-FIRM VARIABILITY OF PROFITABILITY
AND SIZE OF FIRM: UNITED KINGDOM

This section examines the variability of profit rates among different firms in the same size group, i.e. intra-group variability, and makes a comparison of these results between size groups. The hypothesis examined here is that firms grouped as the largest will not have less divergent profit rates than those grouped as small firms.

Our U.K. profit-rate observations are classified into a 3 by 10 matrix consisting of the three years and ten firm-size groups. For each year, the firms were separated into the ten size classes by distinguishing the largest 50 firms, the 50 next largest firms and so on. Thus we have a total of 1500 observations classified into 30 cells each containing 50 observations. We calculate the variances for each cell and undertake operations on these to compare variability between groups.

Since we have constructed samples of equal cell size, we use Cochran's test for homogeneity of variances.* The test procedure is to derive the statistic

$$R_{n,r} = \frac{\max (s_j^2)}{\sum s_j^2} \qquad (7.1)$$

where n is the number of observations in each cell, r is the number of groups, s_j^2 the estimate of the variance of the jth cell and $\max (s_j^2)$ is the largest estimated variance of the j cells. In this particular test, j runs from 1 to 10, $r = 10$ and $n = 25$. If $R_{n,r}$ is greater than the critical level then we reject the hypothesis of equal variability.

The results of our tests of equal variability of profit rates of firms of different sizes are presented in Table 7.1. We do not reject the

---

* If the cells did not have equal observations Bartlett's test or a similar test would have been used and as most of these other tests are sensitive to the third and fourth moments about the mean they require more computation than Cochran's. See Scheffé (1959, pp. 331–58) and Guenther (1964, pp. 20–21) for discussion of these tests.

hypothesis for any year at the 5 per cent level, and conclude for the 500 largest U.K. firms that there is no systematic tendency for profit variability between firms in the same size class to be related to firm size.

TABLE 7.1

Homogeneity of variances:
United Kingdom,
1969–70 to 1971–2

Year	Cochran statistic
1969–70	0.123
1970–1	0.121
1971–2	0.118

Note: Critical value of the Cochran statistic, for j from 1 to 10, $r = 10$, $n = 50$, is 0.163 at the 5 per cent significance level.

Our results here are different from those of Samuels and Smyth (1968) in their analysis of 186 U.K. firms over the ten-year period 1954 to 1963. However, the results do not necessarily conflict as the Samuels and Smyth sample covered a much wider spectrum of firms and there appears to be a tendency for the higher variances to be concentrated in those firms too small to be included in the 500 largest firms.

3 INTER-FIRM VARIABILITY OF PROFITABILITY AND TIME: UNITED KINGDOM

We now compare intra-group variability over time. The purpose of this investigation is to determine if the business cycle affects large firms differently from small firms. Table 7.2 presents the Cochran test for homogeneity of variances again, this time the Cochran statistic being computed between time and variance for each size group over the three-year period. Now j runs from 1 to 3, $r = 3$ and $n = 50$. The hypothesis of equal variability is not rejected at the 5 per cent level for any of the ten size classes. Again this result is different from the Samuels and Smyth (1968) finding that the time variability of profitability was inversely related to firm size. However,

Samuels and Smyth attributed their result to a difference between firms with assets in excess of £2.5 million in 1954 and those with assets less than this, and these smaller firms with the larger time variances are not large enough to be included in our study.

TABLE 7.2

Homogeneity of variances:
United Kingdom,
size classes

Group (largest = 1)	Cochran statistic
1	0.354
2	0.349
3	0.347
4	0.351
5	0.362
6	0.345
7	0.350
8	0.391
9	0.348
10	0.342

Note: Critical value of the Cochran statistic, for j from 1 to 3, $r = 3$, $n = 50$, is 0.465 at the 5 per cent significance level.

4 INTER-FIRM VARIABILITY OF PROFITABILITY AND SIZE OF FIRM: UNITED STATES

We classified the U.S. profit-rate observations into a 9 by 20 matrix consisting of nine years and twenty size groups; thus our 4500 observations are classified into 180 cells each containing 25 observations.

Cochran statistics are given in Table 7.3; j runs from 1 to 20, $r = 20$ and $n = 25$. We reject the hypothesis of equal variability for four years at the 1 per cent level, for four more years at the 5 per cent level, and we do not reject the hypothesis at the 5 per cent level for the remaining year.

Thus we reject the hypothesis of equal inter-firm variability of profits for firms of different sizes. We must now investigate whether or not there is a systematic tendency for variability to be greater for small firms than for large firms as suggested by theoretical considerations and the empirical evidence of Alexander (1949), Dyckman and

Stekler (1965) and Stekler (1963, 1964). Included in Table 7.3 are the rank correlations between size class (the class containing the largest firms being given the rank of 1) and variance within that class for each year. None of the coefficients are significant at the 10 per cent level and there is no significant tendency in signs of the rank correlation coefficients, five of the nine being positive and the remaining four

TABLE 7.3

Homogeneity of variances:
United States, 1960–68

Year	Cochran statistic	Rank correlation between variance of profit rates and size for each group
1960	0.143*	0.43
1961	0.097	0.53
1962	0.102†	−0.06
1963	0.106†	0.27
1964	0.133*	0.10
1965	0.151*	0.22
1966	0.158*	−0.29
1967	0.109†	−0.22
1968	0.103†	−0.21

* Significant at the 1 per cent level.
† Significant at the 5 per cent level.
Critical values of the Cochran statistic, for j from 1 to 20, $r = 20$, $n = 25$, are 0.110 and 0.099 for the 1 and 5 per cent significance levels respectively.

negative. Inspection makes it clear that it is the high variances in the medium-size groups (groups 8, 9 and 10) that cause the rejection of the hypothesis of equal variability for different firm sizes; and hence the non-significant rank correlation coefficients. When we recomputed the Cochran statistics for each year with the one or (at most) two extreme variances dropped we reduced the statistics to non-significance. For example, if we dropped one variance the Cochran statistic for 1960 decreased from 0.143 to 0.085.

To test the hypothesis that the observations causing rejection of equal variability each year were randomly distributed among the size groups we applied a Kolmogorov–Smirnov test; the hypothesis was rejected at the 1 per cent level. We also applied the Mann–Whitney–Wilcoxon test in which the null hypothesis $F(x) = G(y)$ is tested against the alternative hypothesis $F(x) \leqslant G(y)$ where, for the nine years, the variances of all twenty groups other than the medium-sized groups 8, 9 and 10, are considered as independent observations from $F(x)$ and those for groups 8, 9 and 10 from $G(y)$. The null hypothesis is rejected at the 0.1 per cent level.

Even though Stekler (1963, 1964) obtained a significant inverse relationship between intra-class variability and firm size our results do not necessarily contradict his. When our sample is ranked by assets instead of sales, to make it comparable with Stekler's, it may be seen that our smallest firm has assets of $11 million whereas Stekler's has $25,000. Thus our small firms make up Stekler's medium-size firms, and the inverse relationship he obtained came essentially from firms too small to be included in our sample.

5 INTER-FIRM VARIABILITY OF PROFITABILITY AND TIME: UNITED STATES

In this section we compare intra-group variability over time. Table 7.4 presents the Cochran test for homogeneity of variances again, this time the Cochran statistic being computed between time and variance for each size group over the nine-year period. Here j runs from 1 to 9, $r = 9$ and $n = 25$. The hypothesis of equal variability is rejected at the 1 per cent level in four groups, at the 5 per cent level in two additional groups and is not rejected at the 5 per cent level in the remaining fourteen groups. The groups with significant Cochran statistics are group 1 which contains the largest firms, groups 9, 10 and 11 containing the middle-sized firms and groups 19 and 20 containing the smallest firms in our sample.

Table 7.4 also gives rank correlation coefficients between the variances and time for each of the size classes. Only one is significant at the 1 per cent level and one other at the 5 per cent level; the two significant size classes are not among the six groups for which equal variability was rejected. Inspection of scatter diagrams suggests that rejection of equal variability arises through one or two extreme observations, and recomputation of the Cochran statistics confirms this.

As with the United Kingdom, we conclude that within the class of the 500 largest firms the variability of profit rates of the largest are not significantly different from those of the smaller firms.

TABLE 7.4

Homogeneity of variances:
United States, size classes

Groups (largest = 1)	Cochran statistic	Rank correlation between variance of profit rates and time for each group
1	0.211†	0.21
2	0.177	0.06
3	0.143	0.10
4	0.170	− 0.17
5	0.148	− 0.01
6	0.177	− 0.40
7	0.168	0.04
8	0.188	− 0.51
9	0.239*	− 0.24
10	0.393*	− 0.38
11	0.218†	0.39
12	0.174	0.65†
13	0.150	− 0.42
14	0.162	0.23
15	0.187	− 0.22
16	0.153	− 0.74*
17	0.165	− 0.08
18	0.181	0.55
19	0.336*	− 0.08
20	0.239*	− 0.22

* Significant at the 1 per cent level.
† Significant at the 5 per cent level.
Critical values of the Cochran statistic, for j from 1 to 9, $r = 9$, $n = 25$, are 0.230 and 0.202 for the 1 and 5 per cent significance levels respectively.

6 TIME VARIABILITY OF PROFITABILITY, AND PROFITABILITY

In this section, we consider the relationship between the variability of profitability and average profitability over a time period. In an examination of inter-class or inter-firm variability the appropriate measure of the variability of profit rates is the residual variance about trend. We show that the time variance of profitability and average profitability will be correlated if there are time trends in profitability and hence that the residual variance about trend is a preferred measure of the variability of profitability.*

Suppose that the rate of return, π, of a firm is related to time, t, by

* See also Briscoe, Samuels and Smyth (1969).

$$\pi_t = a + bt \tag{7.2}$$

and we have n observations on time periods ($t = 1, \ldots n$). The mean rate of return, $\bar{\pi}$, is given by

$$\bar{\pi} = a + \frac{1}{n} \sum_{i=1}^{n} bt \tag{7.3}$$

If we use the formula for the sum of the first n natural numbers this progression can be summed to yield

$$\bar{\pi} = a + \frac{b}{2}(n + 1) \tag{7.4}$$

Deviations from the mean are then

$$\pi_t - \bar{\pi} = b[t - \tfrac{1}{2}(n + 1)] \tag{7.5}$$

so that, if we use (7.4) and the formula for the sum of the squares of the first n natural numbers, the variance of π_t, $\sigma_{\bar{\pi}}^2$, is given by

$$\sigma_{\bar{\pi}}^2 = \sum_{t=1}^{n} [b(t - \tfrac{1}{2}(n + 1)]^2$$

$$= \frac{b^2}{12}(n^2 - 1) \tag{7.6}$$

We may write (7.4) as

$$\frac{2(\bar{\pi} - a)}{b} = n + 1 \tag{7.7}$$

and combining (7.6) and (7.7) we have

$$\sigma_{\bar{\pi}}^2 = b\frac{(n - 1)(\bar{\pi} - a)}{6} \tag{7.8}$$

Thus the variance of profitability and the mean rate of profit are directly related. If a and b are identical for all firms then there will be an exact relationship between $\sigma_{\bar{\pi}}^2$ and $\bar{\pi}$. It we allow a and b to be stochastic then $\sigma_{\bar{\pi}}^2$ and $\bar{\pi}$ will be correlated, although the correlation coefficient will be less than one. Thus mean profitability and the variance of profitability will be correlated.

In order to remove this effect, we shall make use of the variance about trend for individual firms. Thus, introducing a non-trend term, ε_t, into (7.1), we have

$$\pi_t = a + bt + \varepsilon_t \tag{7.9}$$

and, clearly, if we take the residual variance about linear trend for each firm we have removed the trend-induced correlation between profitability and variability of profitability.

7 VARIABILITY OF PROFITABILITY, FIRM SIZE AND CONCENTRATION

To provide additional information on the time variability of profitability for the United States, we fitted linear trends to our measure of profitability – profits divided by equity – for the period 1963–72 for those firms listed by *Fortune* for 1972. Firms that did not exist for the whole period were excluded but it was not necessary for firms to be in the top 500 for the whole period. In all, trends were fitted to 478 firms: 268 corporations had trends that were significant at the 5 per cent level, of which 108 were positive and 160 were negative.

Denoting residual variance about trend by σ_R^2, we first consider whether profit variability is related to size and fit

$$\sigma_R^2 = g + hX_i \tag{7.10}$$

where X_i is a measure of firm size. The coefficients obtained for h for different measures of firm size, and the t-statistics and R^2s obtained, are given in Table 7.5. Table 7.5 also reports the result of using the

TABLE 7.5
Residual variance and firm size

	Dependent variable					
	σ_R^2			σ_R		
Size measure	Coefficient	t-Statistic	R^2	Coefficient	t-Statistic	R^2
Sales	− 0.127	− 0.57	0.001	− 0.056	− 0.74	0.002
Assets	− 0.143	− 0.55	0.001	− 0.078	− 0.87	0.003
Employment	− 0.264	− 0.57	0.001	− 0.153	− 0.98	0.003
Equity	− 0.057	− 1.26	0.004	− 1.012	− 0.32	0.001
ln Sales	− 281.37	− 0.71	0.001	− 1.852	− 1.368	0.005
ln Assets	− 289.54	− 0.55	0.001	− 2.039	− 1.144	0.003
ln Employment	− 168.42	− 0.35	0.001	− 1.312	− 0.791	0.002
ln Equity	− 364.94	− 0.66	0.001	− 2.595	− 1.369	0.005

residual standard deviation, σ_R, instead of σ_R^2. We also experimented with the logarithms of the size measures, x_i instead of X_i. While the coefficients have the anticipated negative signs none of them are significant at the 10 per cent level. As in section 7.5, we find no evidence that the time variability of profitability is related to the size of firm.

We also fitted regressions in which we included alternative measures of concentration to see if profit variability decreased with concentration. Table 7.6 gives typical t-values that were obtained. In no case was a t-statistic for a concentration variable greater than one obtained. We thus conclude that there is no evidence that profit variability is a function of concentration.

TABLE 7.6

Residual variance and concentration

Concentration measure	t-Statistic
CR_4	-0.39
CR_8	-0.38
CR_{20}	-0.35
CR_{50}	-0.30
HFM_4	-0.43
HFM_8	-0.43
HFM_{20}	-0.40
HFM_{50}	-0.33

8 PROFITABILITY AND THE VARIABILITY OF PROFITABILITY

We now investigate whether or not there is a relationship between average profitability and the variability of profitability about trend. We are here testing a version of the risk-aversion hypothesis, discussed in the financial literature in recent years, that investors require higher returns for those investments that have greater variability in returns, i.e. that the average rate of return must be positively and significantly related to the variability of profit rates.

The regression equations we obtain using σ_R^2 and σ_R are

$$\bar{\pi} = 0.125 - 0.057\sigma_R^2 \qquad R^2 = 0.004$$
$$(-1.26)$$

$$\bar{\pi} = 0.126 - 0.011\sigma_R \qquad R^2 = 0.002$$
$$(-0.862)$$

We find no significant relationship and consequently we find no support at all for a risk-aversion hypothesis.

9 CONCLUSIONS

In this chapter, we have found no difference in the behaviour of profit variability for firms of different size in the group of 500 largest U.S. and U.K. industrial companies studied. In addition, in further analysis for the United States, we found no connection between the variability of profits and concentration and no trade-off between profitability and profit variability.

8 Executive Compensation and Corporate Objectives in the Non-Regulated Firm

I INTRODUCTION

Previous chapters have considered various topics in industrial economics including the choice of measures of firm size and concentration, profitability and the growth of firms. We now turn to an investigation of the fundamental objectives underlying the operation of corporations.

Most of the work on the theory of the firm assumes that firms are profit maximisers. Baumol (1958, 1962, 1967) argued that this assumption involves a fundamental mis-specification of corporate behaviour in an imperfectly competitive world and suggested that the paramount goal of those in control of corporations may not be profit maximisation, but maximisation of the sales revenue of the firm subject to a minimum profits constraint.

In this chapter an attempt is made to ascertain just what variables serve to influence the decisions of top management. In the next chapter we determine whether these goals remain invariant for firms which are bound by a rate of return constraint. This latter type of firm has been the subject of much recent interest in the United States, and the goals which motivate the managers of these firms have crucial implications for the efficiency of resource allocation and economic, welfare. As this type of firm seems to have pressures, and hence managerial objectives, markedly different from other firms we analyse, we consider the regulated firm in a separate chapter.

Our empirical evidence will be for the United States as we have not been able to obtain comparable data for the United Kingdom.

We shall assume that executives are compensated in accordance with the objectives of the firm. The objectives that will be considered are sales and profits. If executive remuneration is a function of profits but not of sales then we conclude that the evidence supports the profit-maximisation hypothesis; if executive remuneration is a function of sales but not of profits then the evidence would support the sales-maximisation hypothesis; and if remuneration is a function of both profits and sales then we conclude that the evidence supports a managerial model in which the firm has a utility function in which both profits and sales are arguments, and we are able to estimate the trade-off between profits and sales.

Previous studies have reached conflicting conclusions so, before reporting our results, we shall briefly survey these earlier studies.

2 SURVEY OF PREVIOUS STUDIES

McGuire, Chiu and Elbing (1962), using executive compensation as reported in *Business Week* and a sample size of 45 firms, found simple correlations between executive income and revenues to be consistently higher than those between executive incomes and profits although both coefficients were significant. By then deriving partial coefficients, they showed the relation between sales and executive incomes to be significant and that between executive incomes and profits to be insignificant. Accordingly they concluded that while profits could not be ruled out as a possible managerial objective the evidence supported a sales-maximisation hypothesis.

Baker (1969) examined the specification of the relationship between executive compensation and sales and profits fitting linear, log-linear and semi-log regressions. Baker's study followed one by Roberts (1959) who fitted linear and log-linear regressions. Baker used a sample of 30 firms from *Business Week* and his regressions were for four-year averages. He found both sales and profits to be significant. These results were obtained using a log-linear model – in the linear model, profits were not significant and in the logarithmic model, sales were not significant. Baker preferred the semi-log model as a result of comparing correlation coefficients and Durbin–Watson statistics (obtained by ranking firms by compensation) and Roberts preferred the logarithmic model by a comparison of correlation coefficients. Such comparisons are, however, illegitimate so that Baker's choice of the regressions yielding both profits and sales significant cannot be supported.*

* In the linear and semi-log models the correlation coefficients relate to compen-

Lewellen and Huntsman (1970) produce evidence in support of the profit-maximisation thesis. They use data for 50 of the largest of the *Fortune 500* firms at three-yearly intervals for the period 1942–63. They have two sets of compensation data, one being salary and bonus receipts and the other a more inclusive measure. Both measures relate to the chief executive. Their study is statistically more sophisticated than the previous studies in that they attempt to correct for heteroscedasticity and multicollinearity by fitting weighted least squares by dividing all variables by total book assets. As will be seen in the discussion of empirical results this may not be the best deflator. Tests by us using similar data to those of Lewellen and Huntsman (for salary and bonus receipts only) suggested that their deflation procedure overcompensated so that heteroscedasticity was still present but, now, with error variances inversely related to the dependent variable. Lewellen and Huntsman find profits to be significant and sales to be insignificant; this result is independent of the compensation measure used.

The final study we survey is by Cox and Shauger (1973). This uses the 1969 and 1970 earnings for 150 chief executives, as published in *Business Week*. Three alternative earnings measures are considered. Cox and Shauger regress the logarithm of compensation on the logarithm of sales and on the profit rate. They find that executive compensation is significantly related to both sales and profitability but the relative explanatory influence of profitability increases as the measure of executive pay used becomes more inclusive.

sation whereas in the linear in logarithms model they relate to the logarithm of compensation. Thus the fact that the correlation coefficient for the logarithmic model is higher than for the linear model (as in Roberts) does not mean that the logarithmic model explains a higher proportion of the variance of compensation than the linear model or that it explains a higher proportion of the variance of the logarithm of compensation than the linear model. Similarly, the fact that a semi-log model yields a higher correlation than does a logarithmic model (as in Baker) does not mean that it explains a higher proportion of the variance of either compensation or the logarithm of compensation – for a method of dealing with this problem see Theil (1971, p. 544). Also the Durbin–Watson coefficients cannot be compared (as in Baker) because the residuals are for compensation in one case and for the logarithm of compensation in the other – if the residuals from the logarithmic equation were transformed from log compensation into compensation it is possible that they would pass the Durbin–Watson test because the transformation is non-linear.

3 SALES, PROFITS AND EXECUTIVE COMPENSATION

The survey in the previous section is remarkably inconclusive. Depending on which study he picks, the reader may conclude that executive compensation depends on sales but not profits, on profits but not sales, or on both profits and sales. We believe that these conflicting results arise from two major weaknesses of previous studies: first, the small sample size that is used in the studies, for – with the exception of the Cox and Shauger study which has 150 observations – sample sizes have been 50 or less; secondly, inadequate treatment of statistical complications, specifically heteroscedasticity and multicollinearity and the illegitimate comparison of regressions with different dependent variables. We use a much larger sample of firms and devote careful consideration to the statistical problems that arise.

Our data are for the year 1971 and are taken from the *Forbes Annual Directory Issue* (1972). Executive compensation includes salary, bonus and directors' fees; it excludes deferred compensation and stock options. It is called by *Forbes* 'total remuneration' as distinct from 'salary'. We also have the total remuneration for the officers and directors of the corporation as a group and, as *Forbes* also gives the number in the group, we can calculate average executive compensation. Data for profits, sales and total assets were also obtained from the same publication.

Our data cover 557 companies. Unlike the companies analysed in previous chapters the coverage is not limited to industrial corporations. The only category of firms excluded are regulated firms; these are considered separately in Chapter 9.

The notation used is as follows: *EC* is the compensation of the chief executive; *EG*, the compensation of officers and directors as a group, divided by the number in the group; *P*, net profits; *S*, sales revenues; and *A*, the total assets. Executive compensation is measured in dollars, the other variables are expressed in thousands of dollars.

As the results for the two measures of executive compensation are similar we shall discuss in detail the analysis for the compensation of the chief executive – the variable used in previous studies – and then report the results for the average compensation of the group.

Our basic model is

$$EC = a + bP + cS + u \tag{8.1}$$

where u is the disturbance term.

We first fit an ordinary least-squares regression between compensation of the chief executive and profits and sales; the resulting equation is

$$EC = 149456 - 0.0788P + 0.0231S \qquad (8.2)$$
$$(43.34) \quad (1.77) \quad (7.42)$$
$$R^2 = 0.211$$

where t-statistics are given in brackets and R^2 is the proportion of the variance of the dependent variable explained by the model.

Equation (8.2) apparently provides support for the sales-maximisation hypothesis. The coefficient of sales is highly significant – its t-statistic is over 7 – and the coefficient of profits has the wrong sign (it is negative). The R^2, while only 0.211, is highly significant and is comparable with what one usually obtains in cross-section regressions. However, there are two major statistical problems with equation (8.2) – there is marked collinearity between profits and sales, and the residuals are heteroscedastic.

The simple correlation coefficient between profits and sales is 0.873, indicating quite marked multicollinearity. High collinearity between two variables, such as profits and sales here, causes estimates of their regression coefficients to be unreliable. Johnston (1972, p. 160) notes three major consequences of multicollinearity. First, it becomes difficult or impossible to disentangle the relative influence of the variables (here sales and profits) – specific estimates will have very large errors which may be highly correlated, and the sampling variances of the coefficients will be very large. Secondly, a variable may wrongly be rejected as non-significant because the multicollinearity prevents us from picking up its influence. Thirdly, estimates of coefficients become very sensitive to the sample data. Because of the large sample size this third problem is not likely to be important here but the others are, and it is clearly vital that we do something about the multicollinearity problem.

We have already, in Chapter 3, considered the problem of heteroscedasticity which arises when the variance of the error term differs among various observations. Here we expect the variance of the error term to rise with executive compensation. We followed the Goldfeld and Quandt (1965) procedure and ranked the sample by compensation of the chief executive, divided it into two, fitted regressions to the two subsamples and took the ratio of the sum of the squared errors. This is an F-ratio with $[(n/2) - 1, (n/2) - 1]$ degrees of freedom, where n is the number of observations in the complete sample. The sum of the squared errors for the subsample with high compensation was larger than the sum of the squared errors for the subsample with low compensation, and the resulting ratio of the sum of the squared errors, 5.82, was highly significant. The presence of heteroscedasticity means that the estimated standard errors will tend to be underestimated, i.e. that the t-values presented in (8.2) will tend to be overestimated.

The procedure we adopted in Chapter 3 to deal with heteroscedasticity was to specify the model in logarithmic terms and estimate that. We tried that here but while the ratio of the sum of the squared errors was reduced it was still significant at the 1 per cent level. And the multicollinearity problem was not solved.

A common way to attempt to handle the heteroscedasticity problem is to assume that the variance of the disturbance term is proportional to some scale-related variable and to make use of weighted least squares by deflating by this scale-related variable. An advantage of this technique is that it is likely to reduce the collinearity problem as well since both independent variables are directly related to size and decreasing the scale relatedness of the variables should decrease collinearity. Lewellen and Huntsman (1970) adopted this procedure. They deflated by assets, which assumes that the variance of u is proportional to assets. This involves fitting

$$\frac{EC}{A} = \frac{a}{A} + b\frac{P}{A} + c\frac{S}{A} + \frac{u}{A} \qquad (8.3)$$

Note that the constant term is suppressed in (8.3) We fitted (8.3) and checked for heteroscedasticity, finding it to be much reduced. However, the ratio of the sum of squared errors was now 1.400 which is still significant at the 1 per cent level. Interestingly we find that the variance for low-compensation firms is greater than for high-compensation firms, i.e. the weighting procedure has overcompensated. Collinearity has, however, been much reduced, for the simple correlation coefficient between P/A and S/A is 0.279.

It is clear that deflating by assets reduces the magnitude of the heteroscedasticity problem but does not solve it. Accordingly we considered the weighted regression

$$\frac{EC}{A^\theta} = \frac{a}{A^\theta} + b\frac{P}{A^\theta} + c\frac{S}{A^\theta} + \frac{u}{A^\theta} \qquad (8.4)$$

Equations (8.1) and (8.3) are special cases of (8.4) with θ put equal to 0 and 1 respectively. We varied θ by increments of 0.1 over the range 0 to 2.0 to see if we could find a specification that lacked serious collinearity problems but yet was homoscedastic. Table 8.1 gives the F-ratios and the simple correlation coefficients between P/A^θ and S/A^θ that we obtain, as well as the t-values for the regression coefficients.

TABLE 8.1

Compensation of chief executive, profits and sales, non-regulated firms: heteroscedasticity, multi-collinearity and t-values of regression coefficients for alternative values of θ

θ	Ratio of the sum of squared errors	Correlation coefficient between P/A^θ and S/A^θ	t-Value of regression coefficient	
			P/A^θ	S/A^θ
0	5.819	0.873	− 1.774	7.417
0.1	4.625	0.835	− 0.880	7.063
0.2	3.693	0.781	0.191	6.689
0.3	2.961	0.707	1.462	6.301
0.4	2.384	0.610	2.928	5.902
0.5	1.929	0.498	4.543	5.502
0.6	1.569	0.391	6.224	5.116
0.7	1.283	0.310	7.877	4.766
0.8	1.052	0.268	9.422	4.484
0.9	1.155	0.262	10.804	4.302
1.0	1.400	0.279	12.097	4.450
1.1	1.691	0.304	13.158	4.548
1.2	1.939	0.331	13.761	4.791
1.3	2.438	0.355	14.824	5.155
1.4	2.909	0.374	15.496	5.630
1.5	3.432	0.388	16.097	6.162
1.6	4.080	0.401	16.648	6.812
1.7	4.795	0.411	17.196	7.556
1.8	5.609	0.422	17.754	8.308
1.9	6.529	0.429	17.338	9.100
2.0	7.567	0.434	18.960	9.929

As θ is increased from 0 the ratio of the sum of squared errors declines and reaches a minimum with $\theta = 0.8$; it then rises.* For values

* The assumption of normality cannot be made simultaneously for different values of θ but even without the normality assumption the test is quite robust – see Scheffé (1959, Chapter 10) for detailed discussion of the sensitivity of F-tests under violations of the normality condition.

of θ of 0.7 or less the sum of squares of the higher-compensated chief executives are associated with the larger variances, for values of θ of 0.8 or greater this is reversed and their compensation is associated with lower variances. The correlation coefficient between P/A^θ and S/A^θ falls until $\theta = 0.9$ and then rises. Almost a unique solution to our problem is provided – we only have to choose between $\theta = 0.8$, which is best for heteroscedasticity, and $\theta = 0.9$ which is best for collinearity. We shall pick $\theta = 0.8$. The ratio of the sum of the squared errors is not significant at the 5 per cent level and the correlation coefficient between the independent variables is acceptably low at 0.268. The regression equation obtained for $\theta = 0.8$ is

$$EC/A^{0.8} = 100108/A^{0.8} + 1.0731P/A^{0.8} + 0.0251S/A^{0.8} \quad (8.5)$$
$$(28.81) \qquad\qquad (9.42) \qquad\qquad (4.48)$$
$$R^2 = 0.651$$

In equation (8.5) both the profits variable and the sales variable are highly significant, but note that the t-value for the sales variable has fallen markedly compared to (8.2).

Profits and sales are measured in thousands of dollars so the effect of an increase in profitability of \$1000 is to raise the remuneration of the chief executive by \$1.073, and each increase of sales revenue of \$1000 raises his remuneration by \$0.025. The chief executive is, therefore, prepared to trade off sales against profits at the rate of \$42.75 to \$1.00. This is a plausible figure.

The results for average compensation of officers and directors as a group is similar. When we do not weight by assets (i.e. $\theta = 0$) we have the following regression

$$EG = 41653 - 0.0195P + 0.0062S \qquad (8.6)$$
$$(41.61) \quad (1.51) \qquad (6.90)$$
$$R^2 = 0.194$$

and heteroscedasticity is marked. Multicollinearity is, of course, the same as in the corresponding equation for the chief executive. The regression for $\theta = 0.8$ is

$$EG/A^{0.8} = 33578/A^{0.8} + 0.2030P/A^{0.8} + 0.0105S/A^{0.8}$$
$$(36.61) \qquad (6.38) \qquad\qquad (6.70)$$
$$R^2 = 0.765$$

and heteroscedasticity is rejected at the 5 per cent level. A \$1000 increase in profits and sales respectively lead to an increase in remuneration of $0.203 and $0.011 respectively. The trade-off between sales and profits is $19.33 to $1.00.

4 CONCLUSIONS

In this chapter, we have related executive compensation to sales and profits. We have used a large sample and have dealt with the statistical problems of multicollinearity and heteroscedasticity. The evidence strongly supports the hypothesis that the remuneration of executives depends on both sales and profits. Accordingly we conclude that the firm has a utility function that includes both sales and profits.

9 Executive Compensation and Corporate Objectives in the Rate of Return Regulated Firm

I INTRODUCTION

For the past decade the implications for resource allocation from rate of return regulation have been a widely debated topic in the United States. Over a decade ago a simple mathematical model of a rate of return regulated firm was developed by Averch and Johnson (1962). The model showed that under profit maximisation a firm regulated by rate of return would have a tendency to pad its capital base by employing a higher capital–labour or capital–fuel ratio than was indicated to be optimal for a non-regulated firm producing the same level of output. Recent examination of the Averch–Johnson model has indicated that the type of input misallocation specified by the model depends on the profit-maximising assumption. Under this system of rate of return regulation, different specifications on the objective form leads to many theoretical possibilities for misallocation of resources. The executive compensation analysis undertaken in the previous chapter provides a unique approach to examining the implications of the rate of return regulated model.

The typical public utility in the United States is under the direction of two commissions which dictate the rate of return allowable to the firm. Intra-state sales to customers and the rates charged for these sales, are generally subject to review by a state public-utilities commission. Inter-state sales and rate schedules fall under the jurisdiction of the U.S. Federal Power Commission. In return the utility is usually granted sole franchise over a particular service territory for reasons justified by the traditional characteristics of a decreasing marginal-cost industry. Whenever a utility's rate of return differs considerably from the allowed rate of return, formal hearings are held in which the tariff schedule is reassessed.

The purpose of such regulation is to allow the utility a less than monopoly rate of return in the public interest but at the same time assure a sufficient return to attract new capital. Additionally this profitability should be comparable to businesses with a similar degree of risk. Thus an important task of regulators is to grant a return between the cost of capital and the normal unregulated monopoly rate of return. Theoretical microeconomic models which depict the regulatory process have interesting implications for efficiency of these firms and are investigated below.

2 MODELS OF RESOURCE ALLOCATION IN THE RATE OF RETURN REGULATED FIRM

The discussion below will parallel models of constrained profit maximisation first made popular in the study by Averch and Johnson (1962) and later modified by a number of authors including Bailey and Malone (1970) and Baumol and Klevorick (1970). We shall do little more here than outline these theoretical works and their implications, as the intent of this section is to assess the empirical relevance of the objective functions upon which they are based.

Following microeconomic tradition, let the utility's output, x, be produced by two factors z_1, z_2. The production process is summarised by the function $f(z_1, z_2)$. Unlike firms in a purely competitive market, the price of the product is a function of output, $p = p(x)$, rather than being dictated in the market-place. Thus the static revenue function that the firm faces is

$$R = p(x) \cdot f(z_1, z_2) \qquad (9.1)$$

The firm is assumed to purchase factors of production z_1, z_2 in a competitive market at fixed prices, c_1, c_2 respectively. Total costs of production are therefore

$$C = c_1 z_1 + c_2 z_2 \qquad (9.2)$$

and the resulting profit function is

$$R - C = p(x) \cdot f(z_1, z_2) - c_1 z_1 - c_2 z_2 \qquad (9.3)$$

which the firm attempts to maximise. But the regulated firm is faced with a constraint on the rate of return where the rate of return is defined as the ratio of net current profit to the capital base. Again, this constraint should provide for a return at least as great as the price that the firm pays for capital, but should not exceed the regulatory commissions' allowed rate of return. This may be depicted as

$$c_1 \leq c_1 + d \leq r \qquad (9.4)$$

where r is the regulators' allowed return; c_1 the cost of capital; and $d =$ some rate of return.

Let z_1 be the invested capital; z_2 the amount of second input, say labour; and c_2 the cost per unit of labour. The formal regulatory constraint is therefore*

$$\frac{pf - c_2 z_2}{z_1} \leq c_1 + d = r \qquad (9.5)$$

or simply

$$pf \leq rz_1 + c_2 z_2 \qquad (9.6)$$

Conditions from differential calculus of constrained optimisation for profit maximisation require maximising the Lagrangian function:

$$\text{max}: pf - c_1 z_1 - c_2 z_2 + \lambda(pf - rz_1 - c_2 z_2) \qquad (9.7)$$

where λ is the Lagrange multiplier. Taking first-order conditions of (9.7) and rearranging gives, where f_1, f_2 are the partial derivatives of f with respect to z_1, z_2 respectively,

$$\frac{f_1}{f_2} = \frac{r}{c_2} - \frac{\lambda}{1-\lambda}\left(\frac{r-c_1}{c_2}\right) < \frac{c_1}{c_2} \qquad (9.8)$$

Recall that least-cost production in a non-regulated firm requires as a necessary condition the ratio of the marginal productivities of the factors capital and labour to equal the ratio of their respective prices, or

$$\frac{f_1}{f_2} = \frac{c_1}{c_2} \qquad (9.9)$$

From equation (9.8), these conditions are not met so long as $r \neq c_1$. And by previous assumption, allowed rate of return must be sufficient to cover the cost of capital, in which case $r > c_1$, and the regulated firm employs a capital–labour ratio greater than would be employed by a non-regulated firm producing the same level of output and

* $c_1 + d = r$ actually need not be a strict equality but will be considered as such here to avoid unnecessary mathematical detail.

minimising costs. From this theoretical result have stemmed suspicions that a regulated firm pads its invested capital base to enjoy greater profits. This is one allegation we test empirically.

Consider the same regulated firm maximising sales or revenues rather than profits. Utilising the assumptions and notation above, profits are replaced by the sales or total revenue function

$$R = pf \tag{9.10}$$

Retaining the same regulatory constraint, the Lagrangian for the sales maximisation is

$$\max: pf + \lambda \, (pf - rz_1 - c_2 z_2) \tag{9.11}$$

First-order conditions for maximising equation (9.4) require

$$\left.\begin{aligned}
pf_1 &= - \lambda \, (pf_1 - r) \\
pf_2 &= - \lambda \, (pf_2 - c_2) \\
pf &= rz_1 + c_2 z_2
\end{aligned}\right\} \tag{9.12}$$

Efficiency of resource allocation may be investigated by dividing the first equation in (9.12) above by the second and simplifying to

$$\frac{f_1}{f_2} = \frac{r}{c_2} > \frac{c_1}{c_2} \tag{9.13}$$

since by assumption $r > c_1$. The conclusions here are the opposite of those of the profit model. As the ratio of marginal productivities now exceeds the input-price ratio, the firm is actually *underutilising* capital, the capital–labour ratio being smaller than for the least-cost ratio given by a non-regulated firm for the same output. Thus, slight modification of the theoretical objective function alters the conclusions drastically. This extreme sensitivity has left both academics and practitioners quite uneasy, since the direction of the entire regulatory process could hinge on the very abstract differentiation of regulated corporate objectives. Application of the empirical techniques demonstrated in the last chapter should provide considerable insight into this matter.

3 EMPIRICAL ANALYSIS

Again we attempt to determine whether top executive and average executive compensation is related to either profits or sales or both.

Should our results correspond to the conclusion of the previous chapter, that of multiple objectives, theoretical analyses have shown that resource mixes are indeterminate for the regulated industries, and no unequivocal conclusion regarding efficiency can be drawn – see for example Bailey and Malone (1970), Baumol and Klevorick (1970) and Boyes (1973).

The data are again for 1971 and taken from *Forbes Annual Directory Issue* (1972) but our sample size is much smaller – it consists of 49 firms. The variables correspond to the definitions given for non-regulated firms. It is not clear, however, that the profit and sales variables assume the same interpretation for regulated firms as they do for non-regulated firms. This follows from the dual role of profits in the profit-maximisation model, acting as both a scale and constraint variable for rate of return regulated firms.

As in the previous chapter, we fit an equation of the general form

$$\frac{EC}{A^\theta} = \frac{a}{A^\theta} + b\frac{P}{A^\theta} + c\frac{S}{A^\theta} + \frac{u}{A^\theta} \qquad (9.14)$$

to try to handle the problems of heteroscedasticity and multicollinearity. Table 9.1 reports the ratio of the sum of the squared errors obtained from regressions fitted to high and low-compensation firms, the correlation coefficient between P/A^θ and S/A^θ and the t-values of the regression coefficients for values of θ between 0 and 2. Unfortunately the specification of question (9.14) does not reduce the statistical problems to the degree accomplished for non-regulated firms. As θ is increased the correlation cofficient falls from 0.998 for $\theta = 0$ to 0.660 for $\theta = 0.9$; it then rises. The heteroscedasticity ratio falls monotonically from 17.010 for $\theta = 0$ to 2.932 for $\theta = 2.0$. Clearly we do not have the fortuitous pattern obtained in the previous chapter when the correlation coefficient and the ratio reached their minima for nearly the same values of θ. For all the values of θ we have, there is still marked heteroscedasticity (the variance of the error term increasing with compensation) and even with $\theta = 0.9$ there is still considerable collinearity between the profit and sales variables.

The collinearity between P/A^θ and S/A^θ and the heteroscedasticity operate in opposite directions as far as the significance of the t-statistics are concerned – the former causing the t-statistics to be underestimated and the latter causing them to be overestimated. However, for no value of θ is the t-statistic of the profit variable large enough to be significant at the 5 per cent level so, unless there is a pronounced downward bias in the t-statistics, we may conclude that the profit variable is not significant. The sales variable, on the other hand, is markedly significant once θ is large enough to eliminate the most extreme collinearity, and remains over 3 as heteroscedasticity is reduced. Unless t-values are greatly overestimated we conclude that the sales variable is significant.

TABLE 9.1

Compensation of chief executive, profits and sales,
rate of return regulated firms: heteroscedasticity,
multicollinearity and t-values of regression
coefficients for alternative values of θ

θ	Ratio of the sum of squared errors	Correlation coefficient between P/A^θ and S/A^θ	t-Values of regression coefficient	
			P/A^θ	S/A^θ
0	17.010	0.998	0.074	0.331
0.1	15.159	0.996	− 0.313	0.721
0.2	13.803	0.992	− 0.686	1.112
0.3	12.810	0.984	− 1.027	1.504
0.4	12.071	0.966	− 1.313	1.901
0.5	11.491	0.927	− 1.502	2.309
0.6	10.990	0.852	− 1.546	2.722
0.7	10.498	0.744	− 1.422	3.111
0.8	0.971	0.663	− 1.169	3.435
0.9	9.404	0.660	− 0.865	3.665
1.0	8.802	0.699	− 0.563	3.806
1.1	8.175	0.740	− 0.281	3.877
1.2	7.799	0.773	0.032	3.932
1.3	6.872	0.797	0.237	3.882
1.4	6.041	0.817	0.441	3.781
1.5	5.214	0.832	0.693	3.684
1.6	4.721	0.841	0.909	3.610
1.7	4.301	0.849	1.166	3.565
1.8	3.842	0.856	1.317	3.517
1.9	3.361	0.862	1.489	3.418
2.0	2.932	0.866	1.646	3.319

Below we report the regression equations obtained for $\theta = \theta$ and $\theta = 0.9$, the value of θ for which collinearity is least.

$$EC = 110419 + 0.0083P + 0.0184S \qquad (9.15)$$
$$(19.32) \quad\ (0.07) \quad\quad (0.33)$$
$$R^2 = 0.487$$

$$EC/A^{0.9} = 82069/A^{0.9} - 0.3862P/A^{0.9} + 0.1716S/A^{0.9} \quad (9.16)$$
$$(8.42) \qquad\qquad (-0.87) \qquad\qquad (3.67)$$
$$R^2 \quad = 0.761$$

The corresponding equations for average compensation of the officers and directors as a group yield similar results. We thus conclude that rate of return regulated firms are sales maximisers rather than profit maximisers.

The non-significance of the profit coefficient may be the result of non-linearities between executive compensation and profits. Firms which approach or exceed the regulator's rate of return may consider the additional profits as undesirable since the outcome may be reduced rates; once rates are reduced there are often long lags in the regulatory process which could harm the firm's financial position if high profitability is short-lived. Thus executives may consider profitability over the allowed rate of return as adversely affecting their compensation package. This is difficult to test directly because the allowed rate of return varies from firm to firm and because time series as well as cross-section data would be needed to properly investigate this dynamic behaviour. To perform a crude test we re-estimated our model with the ten firms with rates of return above 5 per cent eliminated; the relative importance of sales and profits was unchanged.

4 CONCLUSIONS

Though a considerable amount of theoretical literature on the regulated firm is based on profit-maximising behaviour, the approach taken in this chapter does not lend empirical support for this hypothesis. Thus the concern expressed about overcapitalisation in the public utility (as expressed by the Averch–Johnson model) appears to be unwarranted. In fact empirical support for the sales-maximisation objective gives support to the underutilisation of capital hypothesis.

10 Conclusions

This study has used data for large U.K. and U.S. corporations to analyse a number of topics – the relationship between alternative measures of firm size, the growth rates of firms of different size, concentration indices, the behaviour of firm profitability and the relationship between executive compensation, sales and profits. Where data permitted, similar analyses were undertaken for both countries; the results obtained for the two economies were quite similar.

Before summarising our results we must stress that they relate only to large corporations. For most analyses the data bases consisted of observations for the 500 largest industrial corporations for a series of years. Our results may not hold for smaller corporations; however, the large corporations studied do account for a considerable proportion of the economic activity in the industrial sectors of the United Kingdom and the United States. The results may not hold either for the non-industrial sector as our data are usually for industrial corporations – for instance, in Chapter 9 when we use data for U.S. utilities, the results obtained differ to those obtained in Chapter 8 for non-utilities.

2 ALTERNATIVE MEASURES OF FIRM SIZE: THEORY AND EVIDENCE

The first topic taken up was the extent to which the choice of a measure of firm size influenced the results obtained in industrial and business-economics studies. We showed that a high correlation between two alternative firm-size measures provides no guarantee that the empirical results obtained will be independent of the firm-size measure used. The necessary and sufficient conditions for measures to be interchangeable without the results being affected differ according to the type of analysis being undertaken. In Chapter 2, we demonstrated that in studies relating some variable to firm size with the intention of estimating the magnitude of response of the variable to firm size the results will be independent of the particular measure used only if the various measures are proportional to each other. In Chapter 4, we showed that if firm-size measures are used in studies comparing the rates of growth of firms of different size the necessary and sufficient condition for interchangeability is weaker; it is that the measures be linear in their logarithms – proportionality is unnecessary.

To see if firm-size measures are proportional to each other we considered four measures – sales, assets, employment and equity – for the 500 largest industrial corporations in the United Kingdom and the United States. Analyses were carried out for three years for the United Kingdom and for five years for the United States; in addition, data for the 1000 largest industrial companies were used for one year for the United Kingdom. To avoid ordinary least-squares regression bias and heteroscedasticity, orthogonal regressions were fitted to logarithmic data. The results obtained were reported in Chapter 3. They are remarkably consistent both for different stages of the cycle and for the two countries. The hypothesis of proportionality between pairs of measures was convincingly rejected for all pairs except assets – employment. We also investigated, in Chapter 4, the possibility that the measures are related non-linearly in their logarithms and found evidence to support this.

The finding that, for large corporations, the magnitude of response of any variable to firm size cannot be expected to be invariant with respect to the measure of firm size used, has important implications. First, it means that the results of many empirical studies are unreliable as they crucially reflect the choice of firm-size measure adopted. We give a number of examples of the sensitivity of the results of empirical studies to the measure of firm size used. Our results also permit the reconciliation of some earlier studies. Secondly, our analysis makes it clear that future studies using empirical measures of firm size should not adopt whichever measure is conveniently available. The researcher should attempt to make use of the theoretically most appropriate measure. If this measure is not available then he should take into account the biases arising from the use of a proxy. And, finally, if theoretical considerations do not suggest the appropriate measure the researcher should repeat his analysis using alternative measures.

3 SIZE AND GROWTH OF FIRMS

The next topic dealt with, in the second half of Chapter 4, was that of the growth rates of firms of different size. Using data for the 500 largest industrial corporations in both the United Kingdom and the United States, we investigated whether there are significant differences in the rate of growth of firms of different size. We found this indeed to be the case; that the smaller firms grow significantly faster than the larger firms. This means that among the largest 500 firms, concentration is decreasing.

4 ALTERNATIVE MEASURES OF CONCENTRATION: THEORY AND EVIDENCE

In Chapter 5 the conditions under which alternative measures of industrial concentration may be used without distorting empirical results were investigated both theoretically and empirically. We found that proportionality between the measures was required, and demonstrated theoretically that the various concentration indices could not be proportional to each other. We then estimated the elasticities between eight measures of concentration for 390 U.S. 4-digit industries. We found that the estimated elasticities diverged quite markedly from unity (the elasticity required for proportionality). Hence the choice of concentration measure will have considerable impact on the conclusions of empirical studies in which concentration indices are significant explanatory variables. Some examples illustrated this.

5 PROFITS, VARIABILITY OF PROFITS AND FIRM SIZE

In Chapters 6 and 7, we investigated the behaviour of profitability (or the rate of return). Our first concern (Chapter 6) was with whether profitability increased or decreased with firm size and whether or not profitability depended on the extent of concentration in a firm's industry. In light of our earlier analysis, we used all four firm-size measures for both the United Kingdom and the United States and eight alternative concentration measures for the United States (only the 4-firm concentration index was available for the United Kingdom). We also used two measures of profitability – the profits/

assets ratio and the profits/equity ratio. Our analysis covered three years for the United Kingdom and four years for the United States.

We found no significant relationship between profitability and the concentration measures in either country for any year.

We found that whether one concludes that profitability increases or decreases with firm size or is independent of firm size depends on how profitability is measured and on the choice of firm-size measure. It should be noted that in both countries firm size accounts for only a small proportion of inter-firm differences in profitability.

In Chapter 7 the profit-rate data for the United Kingdom and United States were classified into cells reflecting size classes and years. We then investigated to see if the variability of profit rates between firms in the same size class was related to size of firms in that group; we found no consistent relationships. We also used the classification to see if cyclical fluctuations had a differential effect on firm profitability in a way that was related to firm size; we found no evidence that this was so.

For the United States the data permitted further analyses. The residual variance of profitability about individual-firm ten-year time trends was found not to be related to firm size, concentration or average profitability.

We concluded that for the 500 largest U.K. and U.S. industrial companies there is no connection between the variability of rates of return and firm size.

6 EXECUTIVE COMPENSATION, SALES AND PROFITS

The last part of the study, Chapter 8 and 9, provided information on the goals of large corporations by examining the relationship between executive compensation, sales and profits. The analysis is based on the assumption that corporate management is rewarded in accordance with its ability to further the goals of the firm. Most economic theory assumes that firms are profit maximisers. However, there is also the possibility that both profits and sales enter into the utility functions of the firm or of the corporate management. Accordingly profits and sales were the two competing goals that were considered. In Chapter 8 we specified a model that was able to handle the problems of multicollinearity and heteroscedasticity present in this type of analysis and it was successfully fitted to data for 557 large U.S.

corporations. We found that both profits and sales were goals of the large corporation and that there was a trade-off between them. We also fitted the model to data for 49 firms that were subject to rate of return regulation – the previous sample excluded such firms. We found that for these regulated firms the evidence supported sales maximisation rather than profit maximisation. The result has the implication that concern about overcapitalisation in rate of return regulated firms is unwarranted.

Bibliography

Irma Adelman, 'A Stochastic Analysis of the Size Distribution of Firms', *Journal of the American Statistical Association*, 58 (Dec 1958) 893–904.

M. A. Adelman, 'Comment on the H Concentration as a Numbers Equivalent', *Review of Economics and Statistics*, 51 (Feb 1969) 99–101.

C. J. Aislabie, 'Further Evidence on the Size and Growth of Firms', *Economic Record*, 47 (June 1971) 230–44.

J. Aitchison and J. A. C. Brown, *The Lognormal Distribution* (Cambridge, 1963).

Sidney S. Alexander, 'The Effect of Size of Manufacturing Corporation on the Distribution of the Rate of Return', *Review of Economics and Statistics*, 31 (Aug 1949) 229–35.

A. Armstrong and A. Silbertson, 'Size of Plant, Size of Enterprise and Concentration in British Manufacturing Industry, 1935–58', *Journal of the Royal Statistical Society*, series A, 128 (1965) 395–420.

R. J. Arnould and L. B. Fletcher, 'Concentration and the Determinants of Profitability of Large Food-Processing Firms', *Quarterly Review of Economics and Business*, 12 (summer 1972) 19–32.

H. Averch and L. L. Johnson, 'Behavior of the Firm Under Regulatory Constraint', *American Economic Review*, 52 (Dec 1962) 1053–1069.

D. Bailey and S. E. Boyle, 'The Optimal Measure of Concentration', *Journal of the American Statistical Association*, 66 (Dec 1971) 702–706.

Elizabeth E. Bailey and John C. Malone, 'Resource Allocation and the Regulated Firm', *Bell Journal of Economics and Management Science*, 1 (spring 1970) 129–42.

Joe S. Bain, 'Relation of Profit Rate to Industry Concentration: American Manufacturing, 1936–1940', *Quarterly Journal of Economics*, 65 (Aug 1951) 293–324.

Samuel H. Baker, 'Executive Incomes, Profits and Revenues: A Comment on Functional Specification', *Southern Economic Journal*, 35 (Apr 1969) 379–83.

T. Barna, *Investment and Growth Policies in British Industrial Firms* (London, 1962).

J. Bates, 'Alternative Measures of the Size of Firms', in *Studies in Profit, Business Saving and Investment in the United Kingdom, 1920–62*, vol. 1, ed. P. E. Hart (London, 1965) 133–49.

W. J. Baumol, 'On the Theory of Oligopoly', *Economica*, 25 (Aug 1958) 187–98.

——, 'On the Theory of Expansion of the Firm', *American Economic Review*, 52 (Dec 1962) 1078–87.

——, *Business Behavior, Value and Growth*, rev. ed. (New York, 1967).

William J. Baumol and Alvin K. Klevorick, 'Input Choices and Rate-of-Return Regulation: An Overview of the Discussion', *Bell Journal of Economics and Management Science*, 1 (autumn 1970) 162–90.

Haskel Benishay, 'Variability in Earnings-Price Ratios of Corporate Equities', *American Economic Review*, 51 (Mar 1961) 81–94.

William J. Boyes, 'Theoretical and Empirical Essays on the Averch–Johnson Model of the Regulated Firm', unpublished Ph.D. thesis, Claremont Graduate School, California (1973).

G. Briscoe, J. M. Samuels and D. J. Smyth, 'The Treatment of Risk in the Stock Market', *Journal of Finance*, 24 (Sep 1969) 707–13.

Stanley Cohen and David J. Smyth, 'Some Determinants of Price/Earnings Ratios of Industrial Common Stock,' *Quarterly Review of Economics and Business* (winter 1973) 49–60.

Norman R. Collins and Lee E. Preston, 'The Size Structure of the Largest Industrial Firms, 1909–1958', *American Economic Review*, 51 (Dec 1961) 986–1011.

——, 'Concentration and Price Margins in Food Manufacturing Industries', *Journal of Industrial Economics*, 14 (July 1966) 226–42.

——, *Concentration and Price-Cost Margins in Manufacturing Industries* (Berkeley, California, 1968).

——, 'Price–Cost Margins and Industry Structure', *Review of Economics and Statistics*, 51 (Aug 1969) 271–86.

W. S. Comanor and T. A. Wilson, 'Advertising, Market Structure and Performance', *Review of Economics and Statistics*, 49 (Nov 1967) 423–40.

Concentration Ratios in Manufacturing Industry, 1963, part 1 of U.S. Department of Commerce, Bureau of the Census, *Census of Manufactures* (Washington, D.C., 1970).

S. R. Cox and D. Shauger, 'Executive Compensation, Firm Sales and Profitability', *Intermountain Economic Review*, 4 (spring 1973) 29–39.

W. L. Crum, *Corporate Size and Earning Power* (Cambridge, Mass., 1939).

Michael Davenport, 'Leverage and the Cost of Capital: Some Tests Using British Data', *Economica*, 38 (May 1971) 136–61.

Louis De Alessi, 'The Demand for Money: A Cross-Section Study of British Business Firms', *Economica*, 33 (Aug 1966) 288–302.

P. J. Dhrymes, 'Some Extensions and Tests for the CES Class of Production Functions', *Review of Economics and Statistics*, 47 (Nov 1965) 357–66.

R. K. Diwan, 'About the Growth Path of Firms', *American Economic Review*, 60 (Mar 1970) 30–43.

T. R. Dyckman and H. O. Stekler, 'Firm Size and Variability' *Journal of Industrial Economics*, 13 (June 1965) 214–18.

John L. Eatwell, 'Growth, Profitability and Size: The Empirical Evidence', Appendix A in *The Corporate Economy: Growth, Competition and Innovative Potential*, ed. Robin Marris (London, 1971; Cambridge, Mass., 1971).

R. Eisner and M. I. Nadiri, 'Investment Behavior and the Neo-Classical Theory', *Review of Economics and Statistics*, 50 (Aug 1968) 369–82.

Richard Evely and I. M. D. Little, *Concentration in British Industry* (London, 1960).

C. E. Ferguson, 'The Relationship of Business Size to Stability: An Empirical Approach', *Journal of Industrial Economics*, 9 (Nov 1960) 43–62.

M. C. Fleming, 'Inter-Firm Differences in Productivity and their Relation to Occupational Structure and Size of Firm', *Manchester School of Economics and Social Studies*, 38 (Sep 1970) 223–46.

P. Sargent Florence, 'New Measures of the Growth of Firms', *Economic Journal*, 67 (June 1957) 244–8.

Forbes, Annual Directory Issue (15 May 1972).

Fortune Magazine, 'Directory of the 500 Largest United States Industrial Corporations', annual issues.

J. J. Friedman and M. N. Friedman, 'Profitability and Monopoly', *The Conference Board Record*, 9 (Dec 1972) 49–61.

V. R. Fuchs, 'Integration, Concentration, and Profits in Manufacturing Industries', *Quarterly Journal of Economics*, 75 (May 1961) 278–91.

Bradley T. Gale, 'Market Share and Rate of Return', *Review of Economics and Statistics*, 54 (Nov 1972) 412–23.

K. George, 'The Growth of Firms: An Empirical Study', *Australian Economic Papers*, 3 (1964) 65–88.

R. Gibrat, 'On Economic Inequalities', *International Economic Papers*, 7 (1957) 53–70.

H. Glejser, 'A New Test for Heteroscedasticity', *Journal of the American Statistical Association*, 64 (1969) 316–23.

Arthur Goldberger, *Topics in Regression Analysis* (New York, 1968).

S. M. Goldfeld and R. E. Quandt, 'Some Tests for Homoscedasticity', *Journal of the American Statistical Association*, 60 (1965) 539–47.

Michael Gort and Rao Singamsetti, 'Microdata in the Analysis of Profits', paper presented to the 2nd Latin American Conference of the International Association for Research in Income and Wealth (Jan 1974).

Zvi Griliches, 'More on CES Production Functions', *Review of Economics and Statistics*, 49 (Nov 1967a) 608–10.

——, 'Production Functions in Manufacturing: Some Preliminary Results', in *The Theory and Empirical Analysis of Production*, ed. Murray Brown (New York, 1967b).

——, 'Production Functions in Manufacturing: Some Additional Results', *Southern Economic Journal*, 35 (Oct 1968) 311–29.

William C. Guenther, *Analysis of Variance* (Englewood Cliffs, N.J., 1964).

Louis A. Guth, 'Advertising and Market Structure Revisited', *Journal of Industrial Economics*, 19 (Apr 1971) 179–98.

M. Hall and L. Weiss, 'Firm Size and Profitability', *Review of Economics and Statistics*, 49 (Aug 1967) 319–31.

Marshall Hall and Nicholas Tideman, 'Measures of Concentration', *Journal of the American Statistical Association*, 62 (Mar 1967) 162–168.

P. E. Hart, *Studies in Profit, Business Saving and Investment in the United Kingdom: 1920–62*, vols. 1 and 2 (London, 1965 and 1968).

——, 'The Size and Growth of Firms', *Economica*, 29 (Feb 1962) 29–39.

—— and S. J. Prais, 'The Analysis of Business Concentration', *Journal of the Royal Statistical Society*, series A, 119 (1956) 150–81.

Irving Hoch, 'Estimation of Production Parameters Combining Time-Series and Cross-Section Data', *Econometrica*, 30 (Jan 1962) 34–53.

I. Horowitz, 'Firm Size and Research Activity', *Southern Economic Journal*, 28 (Jan 1962) 298–301.

J. Horvath, 'Suggestion for a Comprehensive Measure of Concentration', *Southern Economic Journal*, 37 (Apr 1970) 446–52.

S. Hymer and P. Pashigian, 'Firm Size and Rate of Growth', *Journal of Political Economy*, 70 (Dec 1962) 556–69.

Antony Jay, *Corporation Man*, rev. ed. (London, 1972).

J. Johnston, *Econometric Methods*, 2nd ed. (New York, 1972).

Nicholas Kaldor, 'The Economic Aspects of Advertising', *Review of Economic Studies*, 18 (1950) 1–13.

D. R. Kamerschen, 'The Influence of Ownership and Control on Profit Rates', *American Economic Review*, 58 (June 1968) 432–447.

——, 'The Influence of Ownership and Control on Profit Rates – Comment', *American Economic Review*, 61 (Mar 1971) 161–3.

R. J. Larner, 'Ownership and Control in the 200 Largest Nonfinancial Corporations, 1929 and 1963', *American Economic Review*, 56 (Sep 1966) 777–87.

H. M. Levinson, 'Postwar Movement of Prices and Wages in Manufacturing Industries', Joint Economic Committee, *Study of Employment Growth and Price Levels*, study paper no. 21 (1960).

Wilbur G. Lewellen and Blaine Huntsman, 'Managerial Pay and Corporate Performance', *American Economic Review*, 60 (Sep 1970) 710–20.

Yu V. Linnik, *Method of Least Squares and Principles of the Theory of Observations* (New York, 1961).

A. S. Mackintosh, *The Development of Firms* (London, 1963).

G. S. Maddala, 'The Use of Variance Components Models in Pooling Cross Section and Time Series Data', *Econometrica*, 39 (Mar 1971) 341–57.

G. S. Maddala and R. C. Vogel, 'The Demand for Money: A Cross Section Study of Business Firms: Comment', *Quarterly Journal of Economics*, 79 (Feb 1965) 153–9.

E. Malinvaud, *Statistical Methods of Econometrics* (Chicago, 1966).

H. M. Mann, 'Seller Concentration, Barriers to Entry, and Rates of Return in Thirty Industries, 1950–1960', *Review of Economics and Statistics*, 48 (Aug 1966) 296–307.

E. Mansfield, 'Entry, Gibrat's Law, Innovation and Growth of Firms', *American Economic Review*, 52 (Dec 1962) 1023–51.

——, 'Industrial Research and Development Expenditures: Determinants, Prospects, and Relation to Size of Firm and Inventive Output', *Journal of Political Economy*, 72 (Aug 1964) 319–40.

E. Mansfield, 'Size of Firm, Market Structure and Innovations', *Journal of Political Economy*, 71 (Dec 1963) 556–76.

Matilyahu Marcus, 'Profitability and Size of Firm: Some Further Evidence', *Review of Economics and Statistics*, 51 (Feb 1969) 104–7.

H. Markowitz, *Portfolio Selection* (New York, 1959).

Robin Marris, 'Some New Results on Growth and Profitability', Appendix B in *The Corporate Economy, Growth: Competition, and Innovative Potential*, ed. Robin Marris (London, 1971; Cambridge, Mass., 1971).

J. W. McGuire, J. S. Y. Chiu and A. O. Elbing, 'Executive Incomes, Sales and Profits', *American Economic Review*, 52 (Sep 1962) 753–763.

A. H. Meltzer, 'The Demand for Money: A Cross-Section Study of Business Firms', *Quarterly Journal of Economics*, 77 (Aug 1963) 405–22.

D. Mermelstein, 'Large Industrial Corporations and Asset Shares', *American Economic Review*, 59 (Sep 1969) 531–41.

R. A. Miller, 'Marginal Concentration Ratios and Industrial Profit Rates: Some Empirical Results of Oligopoly Behavior', *Southern Economic Journal* (Oct 1967) 259–67.

——, 'Marginal Concentration Ratios as Market Structure Variables', *Review of Economics and Statistics*, 53 (Aug 1971) 289–93.

——, 'Market Structure and Industrial Performance: Relation of Profit Rates to Concentration, Advertising Intensity, and Diversity', *Journal of Industrial Economics*, 17 (Apr 1969) 104–18.

S. J. Ornstein, 'Concentration and Profits', *Journal of Business*, 45 (Oct 1972) 519–41.

H. K. Radice, 'Control Type, Profitability and Growth in Large Firms: An Empirical Study', *Economic Journal*, 81 (Sep 1971) 547–562.

D. R. Roberts, *Executive Compensation* (Glencoe, Ill., 1959).

G. Rosenbluth, *Concentration in Canadian Manufacturing Industries* (Princeton, 1957).

Robert Rowthorn, *International Big Business 1957–1967 A Study of Comparative Growth* (Cambridge, 1971).

J. M. Samuels, 'Size and Growth of Firms', *Review of Economic Studies*, 32 (Apr 1965) 102–12.

—— and D. J. Smyth, 'Profits, Variability of Profits and Firm Size', *Economica*, 35 (May 1968) 127–39.

Paul A. Samuelson, 'The Fundamental Approximation Theorem of Portfolio Analysis in Terms of Means, Variances and Higher Moments', *Review of Economic Studies*, 37 (Oct 1970) 537–42.

Malcolm C. Sawyer, 'Concentration in British Manufacturing', *Oxford Economic Papers*, 23 (1971).

Henry Scheffé, *Analysis of Variance* (New York, 1959).

F. M. Scherer, 'Size of Firm, Oligopoly, and Research: A Comment', *Canadian Journal of Economics and Political Science*, 31 (May 1965a) 256–66.

——, 'Firm Size, Market Structure, Opportunity, and the Output of Patented Inventions', *American Economic Review*, 55 (Dec 1965b) 1097–125.

——, 'The Determinants of Industrial Plant Sizes in Six Nations', *Review of Economics and Statistics*, 55 (May 1973) 135–45.

R. Sherman and R. Tollison, 'Advertising and Profitability', *Review of Economics and Statistics*, 53 (Nov 1971) 397–407.

I. H. Silberman, 'Lognormality as a Summary Measure of Concentration,' *American Economic Review*, 57 (Sep 1967) 807–31.

A. Singh and G. Whittington, *Growth, Profitability and Valuation* (London, 1968).

D. J. Smyth, J. M. Samuels and J. Tzoannos, 'Patents, Profitability, Liquidity and Firm Size', *Applied Economics*, 4 (1972) 77–86.

J. Steindl, *Small and Big Business* (Oxford, 1945).

H. O. Stekler, *Profitability and Size of Firm* (Berkeley, California, 1963.)

——, 'The Variability of Profitability with Size of Firm, 1947–1958', *Journal of the American Statistical Association*, 59 (Dec 1964) 1183–93.

George J. Stigler, *Capital and Rates of Returns in Manufacturing Industries* (Princeton, N.J., 1963).

The Times 1000 Leading Companies in Britain and Overseas, annual issues.

Henri Theil, *Principles of Econometrics* (New York, 1971).

R. C. Vogel and G. S. Maddala, 'Cross-section Estimates of Liquid Asset Demand by Manufacturing Corporations', *Journal of Finance*, 22 (Dec 1967) 557–75.

A. A. Walters, 'Production and Cost Functions: An Econometric Survey', *Econometrica*, 31 (Jan–Apr 1963) 1–66.

L. W. Weiss, 'Average Concentration Ratios and Industrial Performance', *Journal of Industrial Economics*, 11 (July 1963) 237–54.

——, *Economics and American Industry* (New York, 1961).

——, 'Quantitative Studies of Industrial Organisation', in *Frontiers of Quantitative Economics*, ed. M. D. Intriligator (Amsterdam, 1971) 184–225.

E. Whalen, 'A Cross-Section Study of Business Demand for Cash', *Journal of Finance*, 20 (Sep 1965) 423–42.

B. S. Yamey, 'Do Monopoly and Near Monopoly Matter? A Survey of Empirical Studies', in *Essays in Honour of Lord Robbins*, eds. Maurice Peston and Bernard Corry (London, 1972).

Index